www.JesusTombReview.com

PRINTED IN

www.JesusTombReview.com

THE UNITED STATES OF AMERICA

FIRST EDITION

Copyright © 2007 by The Vision Press

World rights reserved. No part of this publication may be stored in a retrieval system, transmitted in any format, reproduced, copied, edited, scanned, recorded, or otherwise, except as permitted under Section 107 or 108 of the 1976 United States Copyright Act, without the prior written permission of The Vision Press.

Library of Congress Cataloging-in-Publication Data

Sausa, Don.
The Jesus Tomb : is it fact or fiction? scholars chime in / Don Sausa --- 1st ed.
p. cm.
ISBN-10: 0-9788346-9-0
ISBN-13: 978-0-9788346-9-2: alk. paper)
1. Christianity I. Title.

2007924235

Attention: Take 40% off and use our books for study groups, handouts, fundraisers, premiums, or gifts. Please contact the publisher:

The Vision Press
6900-29 Daniels Pkwy #147
Fort Myers, FL 33912
http://www.TheVisionPress.com
SAN Number: 851–755X

DISCLAIMER: The publisher and the author make no representations or warranties with respect to the accuracy or completeness of the contents of this work and specifically disclaim all warranties, including without limitation warranties of fitness for a particular purpose. If professional assistance is required, the services of a competent professional should be sought.

Author: Don Sausa
Foreword: Dr. Diego D. Sausa
Editor: Dr. Jeffrey Clark
Layout Editor: Jody Ortiz
Cover image credit:
-Tower of David by Maglanist
-Jesus mosaic in San Apollinare Nuovo, Italy

www.JesusTombReview.com

We love Him, because He first loved us.

table of contents

foreword .... - 5 -

introduction .... - 15 -

ch1: a storyteller's bias .... - 19 -

ch2: history of the tomb .... - 31 -

ch3: fundamental claims .... - 39 -

ch4: first claim: an unreported discovery .... - 61 -

ch5: second claim: inscriptions .... - 67 -

ch6: third claim: Jesus family burial in Jerusalem .... - 77 -

ch7: fourth claim: Mariamene e Mara is Mary Magdalene? .... - 89 -

ch8: fifth claim: statistical analysis .... - 97 -

ch9: sixth claim: DNA evidence .... - 109 -

ch10: seventh claim: the James ossuary .... - 119 -

ch11: eighth claim: reliability of the New Testament .... - 131 -

ch12: conclusion .... - 141 -

index of names .... - 161 -

index of subjects .... - 163 -

list of illustrations

acknowledgements

supplemental materials

Christ Bearing His Cross
(Source: H. Hofmann)

foreword

The physical resurrection of Jesus Christ is the raison d'être of Christianity. Without it, Christianity might as well not exist because it does not answer the pathetic reality about man's existence: that everything ends in eternal nothingness; or as King Solomon had said, "…all is vanity and grasping for the wind" (Ecc. 2:17, margin). Because no matter how we planned our lives, no matter how we've succeeded professionally, academically, societally, financially and spiritually, our roads always lead us to eternal nothingness no matter which direction we take.

No matter who we are, no matter how wealthy, happy, and contented, nature still aims to kill us and everyone whom we love, either quickly or slowly, tortuously and without remorse – and it always succeeds, one way or another.…

We're in a world that in and of itself leads to tragedy for everyone; a world where all the great political causes, all the great "isms" (that once held so much promise) have failed; a world where, according to the second law of thermodynamics, everything is moving toward collapse, entropy, heat, death; a world that by its very nature needs to be saved and yet a world in which man – with all his technology and science – can only prolong the agony but never end it.…

There is something in us that cries for permanence, for meaning, for stability, and yet all around, everything in nature, in science, in common sense and reason alone tells us that we can't have stability or permanence. That is one reason why the world is filled with despair, lunacy, mental illness, drug addiction, and alcoholism (if you can't solve the problem, then at least numb the pain).[1]

Without the answer to death, life is eviscerated of meaning – all mundane aspirations, accomplishments, endeavors, realities and belief systems including Christianity are like vapor that evanesces into eternal oblivion. That's why Paul states that "if Christ is not risen, then our preaching is empty and your faith is also empty" (1Cor. 15:14). Without a God who is able to answer the problem of death, "Man," as existentialist Jean Paul Sartre

---

[1] Clifford Goldstein, *By His Stripes* (Idaho: Pacific Press Publishing Assn., 1999), pp. 81-84.

rightly says, "is a useless passion," because we either have to become God or have a God who can deliver us from our asinine existence.

Was Jesus Christ really resurrected from the dead? Belief in such a supernatural occurrence 2,000 years ago is not easy especially in our contemporary materialistic societal milieu. But even back then when this miracle reportedly happened, for one of Jesus' disciples, who previously had seen Christ perform miracles and raise the dead, believing in the testimony of eyewitnesses to the actual resurrection of Jesus was hard for Thomas to do without empirical verification (which he did). He declared: "Unless I see in His hands the print of the nails, and put my finger into the print of the nails, and put my hand into His side, I will not believe" (Jn. 20:25).

For today's postmodern materialistic society, where reality resides within the parochial confines of empiricism – skepticism and outright denial of the supernatural such as the resurrection of Jesus is a given. The recent so called "documentary" by Cameron et al about the discovery of the bones of Jesus should, therefore, not surprise anyone, particularly the hundreds of millions of Christians. In fact there seems to be a growing fad right now among movie makers and authors: if you want to make money quick, make a controversial movie or book that attacks Christ or Christianity (such as *The Jesus Family Tomb*, *The Da Vinci Code*, *The God Delusion*, etc.), chances are, according to Bayes' Theorem of probabilities, your business venture will succeed.

"What science cannot tell us," philosopher and mathematician Bertrand Russell once declared before a BBC audience, "mankind cannot know."[2] This statement epitomizes the basic bigoted creed of postmodern scientism. In order for something to be known as real or factual, science requires that it has to be subjected to empirical verification and demonstrability or repeatability. As one (friend) recent graduate of philosophy said, "If I can't see it, if I can't smell it, if I can't hear it, if I can't feel it, then it's not true." Anything that cannot be subjected to empirical validation, such as faith, miracles and the supernatural, are outside the purview of science, and are therefore, for the materialistic

---

[2] Ted Peters, "Science and Theology: Where Are We?" *Journal of Science and Religion*, 31, no. 2 [June 1996], as quoted by Goldstein, *God, Gödel, and Grace* (Maryland: Review and Herald Publishing Assn., 2003), p. 27.

world, unscientific and unacceptable, or to borrow David Hume's words: "Commit it then to the flames, for it can contain nothing but sophistry and illusion."[3]

The main problem with the scientific methodology is that it is inherently tautological. It is virtually impossible to verify the validity of the scientific method without getting outside of the scientific method itself. It's like trying to define the word "science" with the word science or trying to smell your own nose to see if it smells. It's no wonder, one of its major scientific tenets: "survival of the fittest," is by itself a meta-tautology. It's like saying, "those that survive are those that survive." How absurd can that be? Philosopher and theologian Clifford Goldstein rightly expresses this absurdity with fecundity:

Yet what has been the criterion for judging reason? Reason itself, of course!...Yet to judge reason by reason is like defining a word by using the word itself in the definition. It's a tautology, and tautologies prove little or nothing. How fascinating, then, that reason itself – the foundation of thought, particularly, of modern thought – can't be validated.

The problem for scientism and materialism is how can one step outside a system, into a wider frame of reference, when the system itself purports to encompass all reality? What happens when we reach the edge of the universe? What's beyond it? If there were a wider frame of reference to judge it from (God perhaps?), then the system itself would not be all-encompassing, as scientific materialism often claims to be.[4]

The problem with postmodern science is itself, it is not capable of grasping reality outside of empiricity because it assumes (although usually unspoken) that outside of phenomenon (that which can be verified by the human senses) there is no reality (the noumena, reality outside the grasp of the human senses). And that assumption is humanly impossible to verify using empirical science. The irony is, despite this impervious epistemological bigotry, the very foundations of modern scientism are based not on the weight of empirical evidence but on faith in theories that make faith in Creation and the Resurrection dwarfed by comparison. Theories such as the spontaneous generation of life from non-life chemicals, the shocking inherent "conscious" property and nonlocality

---

[3] Norman L. Geisler and Frank Turek, *I Don't Have Enough Faith To Be An Atheist* (Illinois: Crossway Books, 2004), p.58.

[4] Goldstein, ibid., p. 28.

(omnipresence) that photons possess according to quantum theory, the Copenhagen's many-worlds interpretation which states that the universe splits itself into clones indefinitely each time a scientist examines a photon whether it is a particle or a wave, the special theory of relativity which postulates that time slows down accordingly as a particle accelerates towards the light to make the speed of light constant, the Big Bang theory which states, among others, that the universe came into being from nothing (literally from no thing, sounds like the Genesis account of fiat creation), among others – are foundational theories of modern science that are empirically unrepeatable, and yet scientists believe that they are true. In other words, while scientists acknowledge that there is reality outside of empirical verification, that reality should preclude the acts of a supernatural Being despite the fact that the existing evidence in modern science (consisting of, among others, the Irreducible Complexity, Cosmological [the universe has a beginning], and Anthropic principles) does not point to our existence by chance but to a supernatural One who intricately and precisely placed us here in this universe.

Paul Davies, professor of mathematical physics at the University of Adelaide (a non-biblical creationist) states that if the force of the Big Bang had been off by only as much as one part in a staggering 10^{60} (that is 1 followed by 60 zeros), mankind will not exist (Anthropic principle). He explains: "To give some meaning to these numbers, suppose you wanted to fire a bullet at a one-inch target on the other side of the observable universe, twenty billion light-years away. Your aim would have to be accurate to that same part [target] in 10^{60}."[5] After realizing this mind-boggling supernatural accuracy, Paul Davies concludes: "I cannot believe that our existence in this universe is a mere quirk of fate, an accident of history, an incidental blip in the great cosmic drama. Our involvement is too intimate. The physical species Homo may count for nothing, but the existence of mind in some organism on some planet in the universe is surely a fact of fundamental significance. Through conscious beings the universe has generated

---

[5] Paul Davies, *God & the New Physics* (New York: Simon & Schuster, 1983), p. 197, cited by Goldstein, *By His Stripes*, p. 43.

self-awareness. This can be no trivial detail, no minor byproduct of mindless, purposeless forces. We are truly meant to be here."[6]

Donald Page of the Institute for Advanced Study at Princeton University (who also is not a biblical creationist) writes that the odds of human life existing by chance is one is to $10,000,000,000^{124}$ (that is 10 billion followed by 123 zeros), which is virtually equal to zero especially if we consider the fact that the age of the universe was believed to be 10^{18} (that is 1 followed by 18 zeros) seconds (yes, seconds!).[7] Bottom line, both camps (atheistic and theistic scientists) know that reality exists outside of the empirical box. And basing on the evidence that exists in this postmodern scientific world, which system of beliefs now requires more faith, the atheistic belief that life and the universe began by chance or the theistic belief that we are here because there is a Supernatural Being who put us and the universe in place? The point is, both systems of belief require faith, but the atheistic belief requires more faith in light of the evidence.

Since it is highly probable that there is a God who created the universe out of nothing (again basing on the Big Bang evidence among others), then it is also highly probable that that same God can perform other supernatural acts such as the Resurrection. To believe in the resurrection of the God-Man Jesus Christ is, therefore, not delusional or sophistry because if He was who He claimed to be (God), then rising from the dead is no harder a supernatural act than creating the universe out of nothing or maintaining infinite precision in the universe comparable to hitting a one-inch target bulls-eye 20 billion light-years across the universe. And believing in a God who can perform miracles is no more delusional than the belief that we are here in this universe by accident despite the modern scientific evidence that points to a theistic universe.

Belief in a supernatural God is not only supported by current evidence but by history and (note this), prophecy. The theory that life began spontaneously out of inanimate chemicals and the theory that the universe exists by chance are neither supported by history nor by current available evidence. It would,

---

[6] Davies, *The Mind of God* (New York: Simon & Schuster, 1992), p. 232, cited by Goldstein, ibid., p. 44.

[7] Dietrick E. Thomsen, "The Quantum Universe: A Zero-Point Fluctuation?" Science News, August 3, 1985, 125, cited by Goldstein, ibid., p. 43.

therefore, take more faith to be an atheist (borrowing Dr. Norman Geisler's and Frank Turek's conclusions) than to be a believer in Jesus Christ. An honest truth-seeking atheist or agnostic, after looking at current available evidence and history, will have to admit to this. And there are such honest truth-seeking atheists and agnostics out there. In fact, many have become believers because the evidence is so overwhelming towards a supernatural God.

Astronomer Robert Jastrow, the head of the Mount Wilson Observatory and founder of NASA's Goddard Institute of Space Studies, himself an agnostic, is one of those who honestly admit to the overwhelming evidence that points to a supernatural God. He says: "Astronomers now find they have painted themselves into a corner because they have proven, by their own methods, that the world began abruptly in an act of creation to which you can trace the seeds of every star, every planet, every living thing in this cosmos and on the earth. And they have found that all this happened as a product of forces they cannot hope to discover....That there are what I or anyone would call supernatural forces at work is now, I think, a scientifically proven fact."[8] Einstein's contemporary Arthur Eddington, himself a non-believer, after seeing the evidence for a theistic universe, although feeling "repugnant" about it, was honest enough to admit: "The beginning seems to present insuperable difficulties unless we agree to look on it as frankly supernatural."[9] Jewish scientist and physicist Albert Einstein, himself a non-believer in a personal God, said, "The problem involved is too vast for our limited minds. We are in the position of a little child entering a huge library filled with books in many languages. The child knows someone must have written those books. It does not know how. It does not understand the languages in which they are written. The child dimly suspects a mysterious order in the arrangement of the books but doesn't know what it is. That, it seems to me, is the attitude of even the most intelligent human being toward God. We see the universe marvelously arranged and obeying certain laws but only dimly understand these laws."[10]

---

[8] Geisler and Turek, pp. 84-85.

[9] Ibid., p. 85.

[10] Walter Isaacson, "Einstein & Faith," Time, April 16, 2007, p.47.

So is the resurrection of Jesus possible? Of course, because the supernatural is possible! Do we have evidence to support that the resurrection of Jesus happened? More than enough to stand in court and establish the truth beyond a reasonable doubt. There were more than 500 eyewitnesses who saw Him alive after His death. Of the twelve disciples who saw Him resurrected, none of them recanted his eyewitness testimony on Jesus' resurrection even in the face of death. In fact eleven of the twelve died in the hands of their persecutors because of their testimony about Jesus' resurrection, and one of them (John) spent his last days writing more about Jesus' resurrection (and glorious second coming) while exiled in isolation on an island. Why would these twelve witnesses who had nothing to gain and everything to lose were willing to lose everything, even their lives (persistently not only within a span of months or years but up until the end of their lifetime) rather than recant their testimony about Jesus' resurrection? Because they knew it was the truth. They saw, touch, heard, and smelled the resurrected Jesus. Not only that it was the truth, there was something in the truth they found that transcended everything the world could offer. The truth that Jesus of Nazareth was the only One who had the answer to the most paramount problem of man, the problem of death because He was not only a man, He was also God (Impossible? Not in this theistic universe, where photons seem to be "conscious" when being observed and react accordingly, and appear to be in different places at the same time!). That's why the doubting Thomas after empirically proving that Jesus was alive declared "My Lord and my God!" (Jn. 20:28). Is Jesus of the New Testament historical? Einstein himself admits: "I am a Jew, but I am enthralled by the luminous figure of the Nazarene." When pushed whether he believed in the historicity of Jesus he says: "Unquestionably! No one can read the Gospels without the actual feeling the actual presence of Jesus. His personality pulsates in every word. No myth is filled with such life."[11]

The historicity of Jesus was attested to by Flavius Josephus, the famous first century Jewish historian who was a non-Christian (he became a Pharisee at 19 and later became a Roman citizen) narrates:

---

[11] Ibid. p. 46.

Now there was about this time Jesus, a wise man, if it be lawful to call him a man, for he was a doer of wonderful works – a teacher of such men as receive the truth with pleasure. He drew over to him both many of the Jews, and many of the Gentiles. He was [the] Christ; and when Pilate at the suggestion of the principal men amongst us, had condemned him to the cross, those that loved him at the first did not forsake him, for he appeared to them alive again the third day, as the divine prophets had foretold these and ten thousand other wonderful things concerning him; and the tribe of Christians, so named from him, are not extinct at this day.[12]

This book is an in-depth examination of the evidence of the recent "documentary" by Cameron et al that purports that they have (re-)discovered the bones of Jesus Christ. This claim is significant because it is for the first time that, in the 2000-year history of Christianity, somebody has come up with a serious claim to have found verifiable evidence that shows the remains of Jesus Christ. Up until the end of the apostolic age when the professed eyewitnesses to the resurrection of Jesus passed away, none has ever made a verifiable claim against the account about the empty tomb of Jesus. Not even the enemies of Christianity, who would have loved to parade the body or bones of Jesus, could come up with the claim. All they could do was explain away the empty tomb by alleging that the demoralized, disorganized, and cowardly disciples (who were fleeing and hiding from the Jewish religious leaders after the death of Jesus) stole Jesus' body away right in front of the faces of the Roman guards who were guarding the tomb. This theft story by the Jewish religious authorities, Matthew says "has been widely circulated among the Jews to this very day" (up to the time when Matthew was writing his testimony a few years after the crucifixion of Jesus in 31 A.D., Matt. 28:15).

Tertullian who wrote in 200 A.D. reports that the Jewish religious leaders continued to spread the theft story to explain away the empty tomb, which confirms the empty tomb story and establishes the fact that nobody came up with Jesus' body or bones up to that point.[13] Six hundred years after all the eyewitnesses to Jesus resurrection had passed away, the Qur'an came up with a claim that Jesus was not resurrected because He did not die of

---

[12] Flavius Josephus, *Antiquities of the Jews*, XVIII, iii, 3 (Translated by William Whiston, A.M., *Josephus, The Complete Works*. [Tennessee: Thomas Nelson Publishers, 1998], p. 576).

[13] Geisler and Turek, p. 283.

crucifixion but was rather glorified to heaven.[14] But this account was 600 years after the fact, there was no living eyewitness, and there was no way this claim could be verified because there was no evidence that was presented.

This recent claim of finding the bones of Jesus by Cameron et al, however, although 2000 years after the fact, deserves an objective examination because it alleges to have the verifiable evidence to prove the claim. Millions of Christians all over the world understandably would dismiss this claim outright. Why? Because like Paul they would say "I know whom I have believed" (2Tim. 1:12). But Paul was able to say that (and this applies to the other disciples) because he was able to empirically verify the evidence not only that Jesus was alive again but that He was God. This changed him from a staunch persecutor of Christians to a foremost advocate and teacher of the faith. His faith in Christ was not based on blind believerism but on intelligent certainty about the truth in light of the overwhelming evidence that he saw. The same should be true to Christians, skeptics, theists and atheists. Acceptance or rejection should be based on intelligent knowledge of the weight of the evidence and not on a priori assumptions or bias. It should be based on reason and not on passion. For, to accept or reject on the basis of blind loyalty instead of reason would be tantamount to bigotry. And bigotry like persecution, is always wrong even if one happens to be on the right.

This book is an exhaustive examination of the weight of the evidence to the claim of James Cameron and his cohorts that they have found the bones of Jesus Christ. It is intended not only for all Christians, but also for all who seek the truth about this claim and are ready to handle it. It is not intended for anyone who has chosen to disbelieve because for those who have chosen to disbelieve, no proof is possible. As atheist and self-professed anti-Christ Friedrich Nietzsche once said: "If one were to prove this God of the Christians to us, we should be even less able to believe in him."[15] This book, however, will equip the Christian or honest truth-seeker with the informed reason why he or she believes what she believes regarding this claim. The reality of this claim follows the Law of Excluded Middle – there is only one absolute truth for

---

[14] Sura 4:157,158.

[15] Geisler and Turek, p. 30.

every issue: either Jesus rose from the dead, or He did not; either the bones in the Jesus Tomb belong to Jesus of Nazareth, or they do not. There is no middle ground. Either Cameron and his cohorts are dead right or dead wrong. This book will equip you with the necessary intelligent reason why you should believe or not believe the claims regarding the Jesus Tomb. As we are admonished by Peter, we should "Always be prepared to give an answer to everyone who asks you to give the reason for the hope that you have" (1Pet. 3:15).

Coming out with a book on this issue within a few weeks time was an extraordinary task and required an extraordinarily gifted person to accomplish the task. Such is the author Don Sausa. A published author and prolific speaker, with an extremely broad parameter of competent knowledge in various fields at a very young age, which include theology, history, business, real estate, computer science, law, health care, and anthropology – Don has a passion and relentless pursuit for knowledge and truth. He has a knack for getting to the bottom of the issues and master them with alacrity. Equipped with his mastery of cyberspace and communication acumen, he was able to accumulate all the necessary information he needed from various literature, scholars and other possible sources from all over the world (including the FBI), in record time. The result is a stroke of a genius, a must-read volume that enables the truth-seeker to be prepared to answer everyone who asks for reason for his/her belief.

DR. DIEGO D. SAUSA
Author, Kippur: The Final Judgment

introduction

Over the past few years, there has been an increasing public interest in Jesus Christ. Controversial questions about the nature of Christ and the origins of Christianity have been raised in countless documentaries, seminars, and books aimed specifically at the general public. Increasing interest in Christ isn't that surprising; He is, after all, the Man who changed history with His teachings of love and forgiveness. His name has a following of over a billion worshipers, including a significant number of political leaders around the world.

Nevertheless, the media's increasing curiosity about Christ results not only from His vast following, but also from the equally vast skeptical opposition who deny his divinity. Most of the biblically-themed documentaries that are released on or before Easter each year attempt to disprove the traditional view of Jesus and the Bible: that He is the Savior of the World, God in human form, and that the Bible is His inerrant word.

The 'Discovery'

On Monday, February 26, 2007, James Cameron, the Academy Award winning director of the movie *Titanic*, held a press conference and announced that he, along with Simcha Jacobovici and Charles Pellegrino, had found Jesus. This was not, however, the Jesus of Nazareth who physically rose from the dead and physically ascended into heaven some 2,000 years ago, as believed by Christians. Instead, Cameron depicted a very different Jesus: someone who married, had a child, and was buried physically, with His bones placed in an ossuary, or bone box.

Like an academic paper, the press release began by announcing that there was "new scientific evidence, including DNA analysis conducted at one of the world's foremost molecular genetic laboratories . . . [suggesting that] a 2,000-year-old Jerusalem tomb could have once held the remains of Jesus of Nazareth and His family." The press release and the press conference became instant media hits. Evangelicals, predictably, rejected the findings and instantly discounted the documentary without first reviewing the evidence, thus adding further fuel to the growing controversy.

The theme of Cameron's documentary sounded all too familiar, with Dan Brown's fictional novel *The Da Vinci Code* making similar claims regarding the historicity of Jesus' mortality. Cameron's work, however, wasn't labeled fiction: it was depicted as a documentary with "compelling" scientific evidence that would "change history."

Academia Ignored

Scholars, who are usually consulted prior to the release of theories with far-reaching historical consequences, were blindsided. There was no peer review of Cameron's claims, and many scholars felt that their role in reviewing such claims was totally bypassed.

Dr. Jodi Magness, a distinguished professor of religious studies at the University of North Carolina at Chapel Hill, summarized academia's frustration:

> "First let me point out that by making this announcement in the popular media, Jacobovici, Cameron, and the others involved have chosen to circumvent the usual academic process. Archaeology is a scientific discipline. New discoveries and interpretations typically are presented in scientific venues such as professional meetings or are published in peer reviewed journals, where they can be considered and discussed by other specialists.... The history and archaeology of Jerusalem in the first century are far too complex to be boiled down to a short sound bite, yet that is precisely what has happened here. This is a travesty to professional archaeologists and scholars of early Judaism and Christianity, and it is a disservice to the public." [16]

The peer review process in academia is similar to the review process used by Consumer Reports. Products are tested in an attempt to objectively ascertain their safety, reliability, and value in order to give consumers the information they need to accept or reject the product accordingly. Although this is not entirely analogous to the peer review process, it does illustrate the way in which academic claims are tested for factual errors, faulty reasoning, and unwarranted conclusions. Ideally, Consumer

---

[16] Jodi Magness, *Has The Tomb of Jesus Been Discovered?*, http://www.sbl-site.org/Article.aspx?ArticleId=640 (March 2007)

Reports protects those who purchase products, just as peer review protects academic integrity.

In a similar manner, archaeological discoveries that promise the potential to change our view of history should go through as many academic forums as possible to verify the findings; otherwise, there is an increased probability that the public may be misled by faulty research. Claims challenging the historicity of Jesus Christ as a divine person are not merely intellectual abstractions that are easily assimilated into any particular worldview: they have a significant impact on the spiritual and emotional health of countless people. Given that one could argue that these aspects of a person's health are just as important as the physical aspect, claims that contradict the central beliefs of millions, if not billions, should be given lengthy consideration prior to a celebrated release.

Scholars Chime In

The discussion in the following chapters presents the views of experts from across the world who have weighed in on Cameron's film. The aim of this discussion is to conduct a review of the relavent evidence and sources so that the reader can come to a more informed conclusion as to whether the claims of *The Lost Tomb of Jesus* are fact or fiction.

Since this particular documentary is relatively new, there will undoubtedly be a number of new materials available in the coming months regarding the tomb and its contents. As more thorough studies are made available, the contents of this book will be re-examined and updated for a new edition.

Don Sausa

Jewish Tomb at El-Messahney
(Source: Byram)

a storyteller's bias

"The agenda or perceptual context of those doing the recording must always be considered."
-James Cameron, 2007

James Cameron wrote in *The Jesus Family Tomb*, the book version of the *Lost Tomb of Jesus* documentary, that one must always consider the agenda or context of those who record a historical event.[17]

He is correct.

When scholars examine historical records, they review the entire context to see if there was sufficient historical bias to affect the validity of the source. This examination includes investigating the mindset and personal beliefs of the sources that recorded the events of interest. For instance, when the Gospel of Judas made headlines in 2006, the media gave it considerable exposure, because the writings purportedly cast Judas in a different light. Instead of Judas Iscariot the Betrayer, he was portrayed as Judas Iscariot the Hero who acted to fulfill Jesus' destiny. Contrary to the newly popular portrayal, a more in-depth analysis of the writings revealed that the text was written in the second century by a Gnostic sect with an obvious bias toward improving Judas' reputation. In short, it was impossible for Judas Iscariot, or any eyewitness to the first century event to have been the original author.[18]

In the same way, *The Lost Tomb of Jesus* must be viewed with consideration of the source of the claims. Who is doing the research? What do the researchers believe, and could their beliefs

---

[17] Simcha Jacobovici and Charles Pellegrino, *The Jesus Family Tomb*, (2007) p. x

[18] H.-C. Puech and Beate Blatz, *New Testament Apocrypha*, vol. 1, (1992) p. 387

affect their objectivity? While personal beliefs do not automatically negate a hypothesis, knowledge of the belief system of the authors allow critical minds to understand the context of the work and evaluate how the researchers interpret their work, whether their conclusions are results of the weight of the evidence or a priori with their personal convictions, and assumptions thus concocting the evidence to fit the pre-packaged conclusions.

James Cameron

Worldview: Evolutionist
Role: Producer

    James Cameron is a highly respected Hollywood director and screen writer, having directed or produced films such as *The Terminator* and *Aliens*. His last major film, *Titanic*, won 11 Academy Awards, including Best Picture and Best Director. *Titanic* held the number one spot on the box office charts for several months and grossed over $600 million domestically and more than $1 billion outside North America.[19]

    Cameron played a central role in the development of *The Lost Tomb of Jesus* project. As the producer, he had influence over all phases of the filmmaking process, from the development to the completion of the documentary. He likened his role to that of a 'coach,' guiding Simcha Jacobovici and Dr. Charles Pellegrino in bringing their message to the public.

    Despite criticism of Cameron for producing a film insensitive to Christianity, one generally overlooked fact is that he was brought up in a Christian home. He has publicly written about gaining his initial knowledge of biblical history from his days in Sunday school.[20] As an adult, Cameron has had no known affiliation with any church or religious organization. His worldview is based, in large part, on evolutionary theory, which contradicts the literal biblical account of creation.

    In fact, one of his favorite authors is Arthur C. Clarke,[21] a science fiction author known for such novels as *The Sentinel* and

---

[19] Jeff Shannon, "Titanic," http://www.imdb.com/title/tt0120338/amazon (1997)

[20] Simcha Jacobovici and Charles Pellegrino, *The Jesus Family Tomb*, (2007) p. xii

[21] Academy of Achievement, "Interview: James Cameron," http://www.achievement.org/autodoc/printmember/cam0int-1 (2006)

Childhood's End: books that explore the notion that, through evolution, mankind can transcend his current state of existence and eventually become gods.

Cameron's belief in evolution was publicly evident in an August 1999 speech to the Mars Society. He suggested that space exploration will bring mankind "up another notch in the evolutionary ladder" through the discovery of answers to profound questions (including, presumably, whether life exists on Mars) and that mankind could get a renewed sense of self-worth as a species.

> "If we rise to a challenge, we're gonna redefine ourselves, and we're gonna ratchet ourselves up another notch in the evolutionary ladder. In return, Mars will reward us with answers to profound questions and with a renewed sense of self-worth as a species." [22]

After *Titanic*, Cameron started working on natural science documentaries such as *Volcanoes of the Deep Sea*, a film that took viewers 12,000 feet below the ocean's surface. This documentary was released in September 2003 and was well received by the general public; nevertheless, some IMAX theaters and museums refused to show the film. The film suggested that life may have originated from undersea vents: a view that was labeled 'blasphemous' by some Christians after a prescreening at the Fort Worth Museum of Science and History.

Cameron was caught off guard. He was quoted by *The New York Times* as "surprised and somewhat offended" that people were so sensitive to the theory of evolution.

> "It seems to be a new phenomenon, obviously symptomatic of our shift away from empiricism in science to faith-based science." [23]

A few years after this incident, Cameron shifted his attention to biblically themed documentaries, lending his voice and film expertise to a project directed by Jacobovici and Pellegrino. This documentary, *Exodus Decoded*, tried to explain the biblical story of the ten plagues visited on Egypt as the naturalistic result of a

---

[22] James Cameron, "Why Go To Mars?" http://www.space.com/sciencefiction/cameron_why_mars_825.html (1999)

[23] Cornelia Dean, "Evolution on film? Cut!," *International Herald Tribune* (March 21, 2005)

volcanic eruption in Santorini (near Greece), rather than as the miraculous result of God's intervention. Assumptions based on the examination of archaeological relics were combined with CGI graphics to present a visual re-enactment of the hypothesis. Cameron and his group released their film on April 16, 2006: Easter Sunday. Nevertheless, the film's assertions were rejected by scholars.[24][25]

Simcha Jacobovici
Worldview: Orthodox Jew
Role: Director

Simcha Jacobovici is an award-winning Canadian documentary director and producer. The Ryerson Review of Journalism regards him as Canada's top documentary filmmaker.[26] He received his master's degree in international relations from the University of Toronto, and he is fluent in four languages: English, French, Hebrew, and Romanian.

Jacobovici co-wrote the book *The Jesus Family Tomb* and directed the film *The Lost Tomb of Jesus*. He is an Orthodox Jew by faith, thus leading to his curiosity about Jewish history, Jesus, and other biblically themed topics. In an interview with the Ryerson Review of Journalism, he explained that he always thinks like a Jewish person and that he shoots Jewish-themed films because he brings sensibility to them.[27] In another interview in December 1996 with Israeli newspaper *Ha'aretz*, he further expounded his world view and how it intermixes with his work.

> "The three outstanding foundations of my life are my 'Israeliness,' my Judaism and the fact that I am the son of survivors. They are the driving forces behind

---

[24] Hershel Shanks, "The Exodus Debated," http://www.biblicalarchaeology.org/bswbOOexodus.html (2006)

[25] Christopher Herd, "*The Exodus Decoded*: An extended review," http://www.heardworld.com/higgaion/?p=60 (2006)

[26] Chaya Cooperberg, "The Faith and Films of Simcha Jacobovici," *Ryerson Review of Journalism*, http://www.rrj.ca/issue/1998/summer/265/ (1998)

[27] *Ibid.*

> the subjects of my work – oppressed and suffering groups – and the guiding hand that leads me in the manner of my work."[28]

Jacobovici started working with ossuaries when he filmed the History Channel documentary *James, Brother of Jesus*, released on Easter Sunday in 2003. During his research for this documentary, he found that there was an ossuary with an inscription that contained the name of Jesus, eventually leading him to start *The Lost Tomb of Jesus* project.

In the summer of 2003, the Israel Antiquities Authority (IAA) declared the James ossuary inscription, which included the reference to Jesus, a modern forgery and arrested Oded Golan, the original owner of the artifact. Despite these events, Jacobovici still stands by his documentary, defending it as a truthful presentation. Ironically, one of the main assumptions in *The Lost Tomb of Jesus* is that the James ossuary is part of the Jesus tomb.[29]

On Easter 2006, Jacobovici released his next controversial project called *Exodus Decoded*, sparking a debate about the documentary's claim that the miraculous events described in the Exodus story could be explained naturalistically. Hershel Shanks, a colleague of Jacobovici from the James ossuary debacle and the editor of a popular archaeology magazine, *Biblical Archaeology Review*, wrote to Mr. Jacobovici about the problems he found in the film.

> "I loved it. I was engrossed the entire time. It was brilliant. Extremely creative. The special effects were wonderful. . . . Did you convince me? Unfortunately, no. . . . I start from the very fact that you cannot get any scholars to say they agree. That is a handicap. These are very complex and difficult subjects, about which scholars have had long discussions and brought much complicated evidence to bear. Of course, it is impossible for a TV production to consider all this. But the fact that you cannot get major scholars to express agreement creates some doubt... In other words, you are going against the trend of responsible scholarship – not once, but time after time."[30]

Nevertheless, despite criticisms regarding his controversial documentaries such as *The Lost Tomb of Jesus*, Jacobovici maintains

---

[28] *Ibid.*

[29] Simcha Jacobovici and Charles Pellegrino, *The Jesus Family Tomb*, (2007) p. 53

[30] Hershel Shanks, "The Exodus Debated," http://www.biblicalarchaeology.org/bswbOOexodus.html (2006)

that his job as a journalist and filmmaker is to present issues to the public and not necessarily to substantiate them.

> "My job is to tell the story. To report on it. I don't have to prove anything." [31]

Dr. Charles Pellegrino

Worldview: Agnostic

Role: Co-author

Dr. Charles Pellegrino is a writer of science fiction and nonfiction books. He received his doctorate in paleobiology from Victoria University of Wellington, New Zealand. Beginning with his visit to the *Titanic* wreck, archaeology became one of his favorite fields of science.[32] One of Pellegrino's first published books relating to biblical archaeology was *Return to Sodom and Gomorrah*, which attempted to use science to prove that Sodom and Gomorrah existed, but that God was not the cause of its destruction.

On December 7, 1999, almost 8 years before the release of *The Lost Tomb of Jesus*, an Amazon.com user prophetically recognized that if Pellegrino's thought processes were to be applied to the Gospels, he would probably assume that Christ was never resurrected from the dead.

> "This waffley book is a highly conjectured attempt to [demystify] the Old Testament – and the questionable theology employed throughout doesn't help. If the author were to take a similar approach with the [Gospels], I suspect he would take the view that Christ was never resurrected from the dead." [33]

Pellegrino is a self-described agnostic who considers doubt to be the basis of science. In his view, his role as a scientist requires

---

[31] Discovery Channel, "The Lost Tomb of Jesus: Simcha Interview - Part 3," http://dsc.discovery.com/beyond/player.html (February 2007)

[32] Charles Pellegrino, http://www.charlespellegrino.com/cp_biography.htm (December 2006)

[33] Edouard Chidna, "What happened to the pillars of salt?," http://www.amazon.com/ (December 1999)

him to attempt to explain faith's miracles as remarkable coincidences.[34]

Dr. James D. Tabor
Worldview: Hebrew-Biblical Theist
Role: Consultant

Dr. James D. Tabor is a professor and the Chair of the Department of Religious Studies at the University of North Carolina at Charlotte. He has authored a number of books including *Things Unutterable* in 1986, *A Noble Death* in 1992 and, most recently, *The Jesus Dynasty* in 2006. He earned a doctorate in biblical studies from the University of Chicago.

Tabor has changed his fundamental beliefs a number of times with regard to his theological outlook. According to a published letter, he claimed to have grown up in the Church of Christ and to have spent a year doing mission work in Europe after graduating from Abilene Christian University with a bachelor of arts in Greek and biblical studies. During his time at the University of Chicago, Tabor wrote that his faith in the veracity of the Bible and the existence of God waned.

> "I spent the next decade at the University of Chicago getting first a second M.A., then finally a Ph.D. I was exposed to the most radical historical-critical biblical studies and gradually lost all faith in God, the Bible, or any idea of ultimate human purpose. . . . I would characterize myself as a romanticized, bohemian, existentialist, nihilist - basically a follower of Freud and Nietzsche."[35]

Tabor has also claimed that he has recently begun a return to faith, albeit in unorthodox beliefs and by an unorthodox method. His current beliefs, although theistic, leave no room for the orthodox beliefs of Christianity, specifically with regard to the centrality of Jesus.

---

[34] Charles Pellegrino, "Some facts," http://www.amazon.com/ (March 6, 2007)

[35] James D. Tabor, Published letter, http://www.hwarmstrong.com/ar/AR41.html (March 1989)

> "Just about two years ago, . . . I began to turn back . . . toward faith once again in the God of the Bible, and even in the Bible itself, but in a non-fundamentalist way. . . . But my foundational beginning is the fundamental revelation of God in the Bible, primarily the Hebrew Bible (OT), at least as a starting point. I don't like labels, neither Jewish (which I am certainly not), nor Christian (since I think what Jesus of Nazareth was all about has so precious little to do with Christianity). This return to faith really means simply that out of all the philosophical options I have considered, the one I find most compelling is the claim of God as revealed in the Bible."[36]

As early as 1996, Tabor expressed interest in the 1980 archaeological excavation of the ossuaries that are now the subject of the *Lost Tomb of Jesus* controversy.[37] In a post to a discussion forum hosted by the Orion Center for the Study of the Dead Sea Scrolls and Associated Literature at Hebrew University of Jerusalem, Tabor suggested that the ossuary may have been that of Jesus Christ. While he did not make any explicit conclusions, he did implicitly suggest the possibility.

> "Although we all know the names [Jesus, Joseph, and Mary] are common, it does seem that their presence in a single site should have been at least publicized and discussed when they were discovered in 1980."[38]

Although Tabor claims to be a theist, he is by no means, as shown by his own writings, a Christian. Even his assertion that he relies upon the Hebrew Bible is subject to qualification to the point that his theological views may be considered either speculative or arbitrary.

Understanding Bias

The four main architects of *The Lost Tomb of Jesus* have backgrounds in film, journalism, science, and religious studies. Their worldviews include evolutionism, Orthodox Judaism, agnosticism, and Hebrew-biblical theism. Naturally, the authors' worldviews deny Christ's bodily resurrection: to them it is

---

[36] *Ibid.*

[37] James Tabor, Discussion thread, http://orion.huji.ac.il/orion/archives/1996a/msg00145.html (April 3, 1996)

[38] *Ibid.*

unscientific because it is supernatural, or it is against Jewish faith because Jesus was not the Messiah, or it is untenable because Jesus was not truly the center of Christianity. This could explain why the traditional Christian view of Jesus' resurrection, that He both rose from the dead physically and ascended into heaven physically, was never considered in the documentary to even be a possibility.

Additionally, conflicts between good filmmaking and good journalism were apparent in the film. The director's goal, seemingly, was to strike a balance between entertainment and journalism. Good journalism gives equal time to both sides of the story; this two-hour documentary offered, at best, a few minutes of the opposing traditional view.

All researchers (theists, atheists, Christians, evolutionists, etc.) bring some sort of subjectivity to their studies, but it doesn't automatically mean that truth cannot be possibly presented because of the researchers' bias. A teacher who has a child as his student can possibly give a favorable grade to his child, but it is also possible that the demand for high level of professionalism and ethics would drive the teacher to even treat his child with the highest objectivity to earn the respect of his students and colleagues. Similarly, an ethical and objective researcher is capable of arriving at valid and plausible conclusions basing on the weight of evidence and not on personal assumptions or persuasions.

The film deserves a fair academic response, despite the producers' choice to bypass the process of peer review. Rather than looking at the documentary as an attack on Christianity or as solely the result of a desire for financial gain, it should be viewed as an interpretation, however valid or invalid, of the evidence that was examined.

James, Brother of Jesus ossuary
(Source: Copyright © 2005 By P. Paradiso)

On June 18, 2003 a committee from Israel's IAA declared that the James ossuary inscription was a modern forgery. On December 29, 2004, the Israeli justice ministry charged Golan, three other Israelis, and one Palestinian with running a forgery ring that had been operating for more than 20 years.

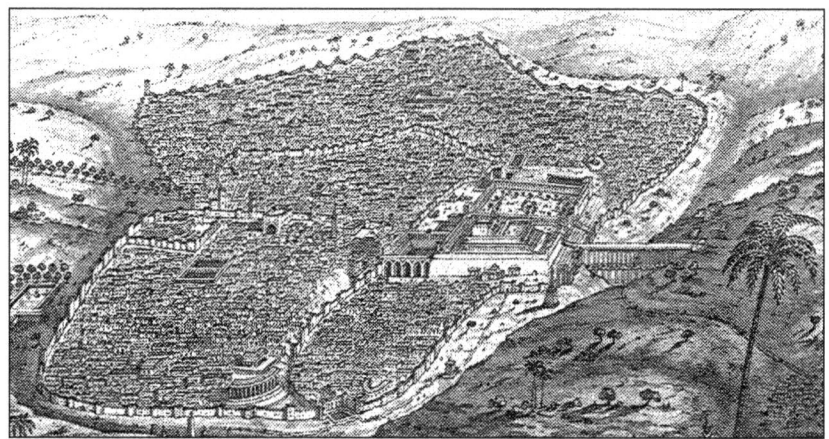

Ancient Jerusalem
(Source: L.N. Rosenthal)

Chapter One: A Storyteller's Bias

STUDY QUESTIONS:

1. What are the similarities between *Exodus Decoded* and *The Lost Tomb of Jesus*?

2. Why are these controversial works released on or right before major Christian holidays like Easter?

3. After some Christians called James Cameron's scientific documentaries blasphemous for the promotion of evolution, why did he start producing controversial documentaries about the Bible?

2

history of the tomb

"We will look like fools if we go down this path."
-Dr. Amos Kloner, 1980

East Talpiot is a suburb that lies approximately three miles east of Jerusalem. The name of this neighborhood in Israel has become virtually synonymous with the recent controversy over a number of ossuaries, or bone boxes, unearthed in 1980 (Ossuaries were limestone boxes where exhumed remains of important persons were stored a year after their death. This was a Jewish custom that started from first century BC through second century AD). During excavation prior to the planned construction of an apartment block, the entrance to a burial cave was accidentally discovered. Ten ossuaries with characteristics that indicated a possible first century origin were uncovered.

In accordance with the law in Israel, albeit to the chagrin of the construction company, the find was reported, and the Israel Antiquities Authority (IAA) dispatched a team of archaeologists that included Amos Kloner, Shimon Gibson, and the late Joseph Gat. (This was not, however, before some local children destroyed some of the skulls, and possibly other artifacts, from in or around the tomb.)[39] Gibson surveyed the tomb and made a number of drawings detailing its structure and layout. The IAA reported that the ten cataloged ossuaries found within were of "no particular significance" and then proceeded to place them in open storage.

---

[39] Simcha Jacobovici and Charles Pellegrino, *The Jesus Family Tomb*, (2007) p. 4

Construction of the apartment complex resumed, and the tomb was covered.

Contents of the Tomb

The condition of the interior of the tomb in East Talpiot indicated that, at some point in the ancient past, its contents had been disturbed, possibly by looters or vandals.[40] The *kokhim*, or small inset chambers in the tomb carved as storage locations for the ossuaries, did not have the expected large sealing stones, which were not found anywhere in the tomb. Also, bone fragments from skulls and limbs, along with two ossuary lids, were found scattered on the floor of the room. Some of the ten ossuaries found in the *kokhim* were broken.[41]

The ossuaries uncovered in the tomb were regarded by Dr. Amos Kloner, in a report published in the Israeli periodical *Atiquot*, as "typical Jewish ossuaries of the first century [A.D.]."[42] Kloner's report was published in 1996 and was based on the notes of archaeologist Joseph Gat. Six of the ten ossuaries bore inscriptions, five in Hebrew and one in Greek. According to Kloner's report cataloging the ossuaries, the inscriptions included the names *Mariamene e Mara* (translated as "Maria the Master"[43] or "Maria and Martha"), *Yehuda bar Yeshua* ("Judah, son of Jesus"), *Matya* ("Matthew"), *Yeshua bar Yehosef* ("Jesus, son of Joseph"), *Yose* ("Joseph" or "Jose"), and *Marya* ("Mary"). The remaining four ossuaries either were plain or, in one case, had some illegible markings.

The *Mariamene e Mara* inscription was written on the ossuary in Greek. The other five, all bearing Hebrew symbols, were inscribed in either Hebrew or Aramaic, a Semitic language used by the Jews during the Babylonian captivity and was a popular carry-over language in Palestine in Jesus' time. The ossuaries bearing the names *Yehuda bar Yeshua* and *Yeshua bar Yehosef* were inscribed in Aramaic; the remaining three were inscribed in Hebrew.[44]

---

[40] *Ibid.*, p. 9

[41] Amos Kloner, "A Tomb with Inscribed Ossuaries in East Talpiyot, Jerusalem," *Atiquot*, Vol. 29 (1996)

[42] *Ibid.*

[43] *Ibid.*

[44] "The First Discovery," http://www.jesusfamilytomb.com/essential_facts/1980_discovery.html (2007)

The names inscribed on the ossuaries were described by Kloner as being some of the most common Jewish names of first century Israel. He states that *Mariamene*, a variation of the name Mary or Miriam, and *Mara*, a contraction of the name Martha, were among the most common names of Jewish women at that time. Furthermore, at least 20 recovered ossuaries from other sites bore the name *Mariamene*. Kloner also identifies *Yehuda*, or Judah, as the third most common name in the Hellenistic and Roman period, and that *Yeshua*, or Jesus (alternatively, Joshua), was the sixth most common name of the same era (first-century Palestine).

Additionally, *Yose* (Joseph) is reckoned as the second most common name in the Second Temple period. Along with the common name *Matya* (Matthew), this list of names inscribed on the ossuaries led Kloner to no substantial conclusions about the specific identities of those entombed.

Findings Published

In addition to Kloner's 1996 report in *Atiquot*, a number of other publications mentioned or delved into the subject of the Talpiot tomb excavation and contents. A 1981 report documenting the findings in the tomb was included in *Hadashot Arkheologiyot*, a journal published since 1961 by the Israel Department of Antiquities and Museums (IDAM) (which later became the IAA). The Kloner publication referenced material from this report as well as from a 1994 publication by Levy Yitzhak Rahmani, *A Catalogue of Jewish Ossuaries in the Collections of the State of Israel*, which included listings of the Talpiot ossuaries.

An article entitled "The Tomb That Dare Not Speak Its Name" was featured in the News Review section of *The Sunday Times* newspaper in the United Kingdom on March 31, 1996. This article, with its provocative title, delved into the Talpiot tomb with popular sensationalism.

One week following publication of the article, a BBC documentary in the *Heart of the Matter* series aired on television on Easter Sunday of 1996. This documentary, entitled "The Body in Question," also examined the Talpiot findings and examined the question regarding whether the ossuary inscribed with *Yeshua bar Yosef* (Jesus, son of Joseph) might actually be the ossuary of Jesus Christ himself, and the other ossuaries those of his family members. Nevertheless, Motti Neiger, spokesman for the IAA, stated that the idea was virtually impossible.

> "The archeological evidence shows that chances of these being the actual [final resting places] of the holy family are almost nil."[45]

The article in *The Sunday Times* and the documentary on the BBC both brought out the possibility that these ossuaries were those of Jesus and his family, in spite of the high frequency of use of every name found inscribed on the boxes. Even in the face of the IAA's determination in 1980 that the Talpiot ossuaries were of "no particular significance," the documentary cited anthropologist and IAA Senior Curator of Archaeology and Anthropology Joe Zias as saying, "The combination of names is really impressive." [46]

Other headlines on the subject included "Holy Family Tomb Find Discounted" in the April 1, 1996 City Edition section of *The Irish Times* and "Coffin in Israel Is Not That of Jesus' Family, Experts Say" in the April 3, 1996 First Edition section of *USA Today*. Also in 1996, in response to Dr. James D. Tabor's previously mentioned posting on an Orion Center at Hebrew University discussion board, several scholars, including Drs. Dale M. Cannon, Kevin D. Johnson, and Niels Peter Lemche, dismissed the suggestion that the ossuaries belonged to Jesus and his family.[47]

The subject of the Talpiot ossuaries was broached once again in 2003 in the book *Excavating Jesus* by Jonathan L. Reed and John Dominic Crossan. The authors raise the subject of the ossuaries and dismiss the collection of inscribed names as 'coincidental.' [48] Also, the ossuaries were discussed by Michael S. Heiser, former professor in the Department of Religious Studies at Grace College in Indiana, in a paper presented at the 2003 annual meeting of the Near East Archaeological Society. The paper, entitled "The Jesus Ossuary: A Critical Examination," presented an evaluation of the evidence from the find and concluded with a dismissal of the notion that Jesus Christ was entombed in a talpiot ossuary.

---

[45] Motti Neiger, http://www.aomin.org/index.php?itemid=1787 (1996)

[46] "The Tomb That Dare Not Speak Its Name," *The Sunday Times* (UK), (March 31, 1996)

[47] Discussion thread, http://orion.huji.ac.il/orion/archives/1996a/threads.html#00145 (April 1996)

[48] Jonathan L. Reed, "In Response to Tabor," http://www.sbl-site.org/Article.aspx?ArticleId=657

2007: Was the Talpiot Tomb Reported?

Given the number of publications discussing both the Talpiot ossuaries and the proposed possibility that they bore the remnants of Jesus Christ and his family, it is clear that the book *The Jesus Family Tomb* and the corresponding documentary, *The Lost Tomb of Jesus*, do not present any breaking news. Stories proclaiming the possible discovery of Jesus' remains, or at least the box that was marked with his name and, presumably, that carried his bones, have circulated in popular media outlets for over a decade.

The list of popular articles, books, scholarly publications, and Internet discussion board exchanges, along with the BBC documentary, quite clearly show that the Talpiot find is news by no means. Only by ignoring the public and widely-read interaction between journalists, experts, and scholars can one come to the conclusion that there was some form of cover-up or obfuscation with regard to the 1980 discovery. The list of those scholars who reject the ossuary inscriptions as coincidental or insignificant is certainly not limited to those who hold to orthodox Christianity; indeed, many of those who reject the sensational headlines associated with the controversy have no particular love for the notion of Jesus Christ as divine or as having physically risen from the dead.

Chapter Two: History of the Tomb

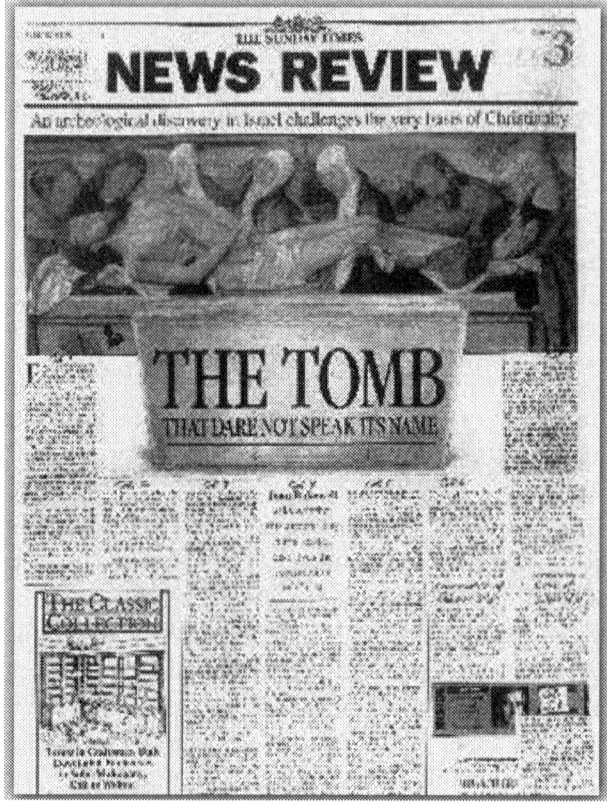

Headline from the News Review of the Sunday Times *of the United Kingdom.*
(Source: *The Sunday Times*)

On March 31, 1996, the *Sunday Times* published an article entitled "The Tomb That Dare Not Speak Its Name," partly in anticipation of the upcoming BBC documentary made for the *Heart of the Matter* series and entitled "The Body in Question." With some level of sensationalism, the article suggested that the ossuaries found in East Talpiot in 1980 may just have been those of Jesus Christ and his relatives.

Tomb of the Kings
(Source: Byram)

Chapter Two: History of the Tomb

STUDY QUESTIONS:

1. How common was the name Jesus during the first century?

2. What type of fragments were scattered all over the floor?

3. What do you think the purpose was of the stone covers were for *kokhim* shafts? What does it mean to you if the covers were missing in a tomb?

3

fundamental claims

> *"The Discovery, the Investigation, and the Evidence That Could Change History."*
> -Simcha Jacobovici and Charles Pellegrino, 2007

The case made in the book *The Jesus Family Tomb* and corresponding documentary, *The Lost Tomb of Jesus*, involves a collection of claims, each of which may be unimpressive but, when combined, together may become convincing. To recognize the justification for the conclusion that the Talpiot tomb is very likely the burial place of Jesus Christ, one must first recognize all the major claims that are foundational to this conclusion. The argument is only as acceptable as the claims made in support of it.

The conclusion of any valid argument rests upon the foundation of the premises that support it. For valid deductive arguments, the conclusion necessarily follows, if the premises, or fundamental claims, are true. If any of the relevant claims or premises is shown to be false, however, the conclusion becomes unwarranted and cannot be reasonably maintained.

For inductive arguments, such as are more often used in archaeology with regard to historical possibilities and explanations, conclusions are built on evidence that is collected in an attempt to gain greater and greater confidence in a hypothesis. As a result, the acceptability of the conclusion may not rest on the strength of each claim, but instead on the combined strength of all the supporting claims together.

The case for the thesis that East Talpiot was the final resting place of the bones of Jesus Christ is an inductive argument. By bringing to bear a number of individual facts, the writers attempt to slowly build up confidence in the thesis. If the premises, or supporting claims, are found to be faulty, confidence in the conclusion is diminished. The strength of the argument, therefore, is wholly dependent on the truthfulness of the combination of supporting claims.

First Claim: An Unreported Discovery

Although the question of whether the story has been widely reported is not a critical issue in making the case for the identity of those once entombed in the Talpiot ossuaries, it does bring to bear certain rhetorical force. If those who first explored the tomb were attempting to quiet speculation or further investigation into what could be evidence for a staggering discovery, then a new presentation of the facts gains the kind of urgency and freshness that is associated with a breaking news story. Furthermore, it brings into question the motivations, and even integrity, of those who were apparently unwilling to discuss or publicize information about the find.

On several occasions in the recent book and documentary, the claim was made that the Talpiot tomb, along with its curiously inscribed ossuaries, was kept hidden from both the public and from other scholars. The narration of the documentary, *The Lost Tomb of Jesus*, included a statement that implicitly suggested a conspiracy.

> "We've assembled a team of scientists, scholars, and journalists to investigate the ten ancient bone boxes to find out why they've been ignored."[49]

Also, the narrator asked a rhetorical question with a similar effect.

> "Why didn't anyone take notice of [the names on the ossuaries]?"[50]

---

[49] *The Lost Tomb of Jesus*, The Discovery Channel (2007)
[50] *Ibid.*

In addition to those portions of the narration that implicitly suggested either ignorance or deceit on the part of the archaeologists (and others) involved in the discovery of the tomb in 1980, Dr. James D. Tabor suggested in an interview segment that the public was unaware of the discovery, at least at the time it was made.

> "When [the ossuary with the inscription *Yeshua bar Yehosef*] was found, I think the archaeologists weren't too excited about it. The public would've been very excited about it, but they didn't hear about it. 'They found a Jesus, son of Joseph ossuary?' But it wasn't really talked about."[51]

While relating a 2003 discussion with the above-mentioned Tabor, Simcha Jacobovici unequivocally stated in *The Jesus Family Tomb* that most scholars were unaware of the Talpiot find and its controversial contents.

> "Most scholars had no idea the [Talpiot] tomb existed."[52]

Jacobovici also made a similar comment in a trailer for the documentary, suggesting that the find either went ignored or went unnoticed by archaeologists and other scholars.

> "This is a site that's fallen between the archaeological cracks."[53]

There can be no doubt that the documentary and book about the contents of the Talpiot tomb present the case in light of the belief that not only have the findings not yet been sufficiently examined, but that they are not even known to most scholars and archaeologists. As mentioned previously, this does not necessarily provide evidence for or against the conclusions presented, but it does provide a certain aura of mystery and intrigue that may make controversial findings somewhat more acceptable, psychologically at least, to viewers and readers.

Second Claim: Controversial Inscriptions

---

[51] *Ibid.*

[52] Simcha Jacobovici and Charles Pellegrino, *The Jesus Family Tomb* (2007) p. 52

[53] Trailer for *The Lost Tomb of Jesus*, http://www.jesusfamilytomb.com/trailer.html (2007)

Chapter Three: Fundamental Claims

One of the most fundamental claims made in *The Jesus Family Tomb* involves the readings of the inscriptions on two of the ossuaries from the find. The claim of the authors is that one of the ossuaries, which is otherwise plain and unremarkable, bears the Aramaic name *Yeshua bar Yehosef*, or "Jesus, son of Joseph." The other ossuary, inscribed in Greek, is said to bear the name *Mariamene e Mara*, which the authors translate as "Mariamne (or Mary), the Master."

The readings and translations of these two inscriptions are fundamental to the major, and most controversial, claims of the book. With regard to *Yeshua bar Yosef*, the authors claim that this inscription is clearly determined by examination of the otherwise plain ossuary, despite the difficulties reading the inscription.

> "'Jesus, son of Joseph.' Hard to read, but, in the end, easily decipherable."[54]

Frank Moore Cross, Jr., Hancock Professor of Hebrew and Other Oriental Languages Emeritus at Harvard Divinity School, also attests to the same reading in *The Lost Tomb of Jesus*.

> "I have no real doubt that this is to be read *Yeshua*, and then *Yeshua bar Yehosef*, that is 'Jesus, son of Joseph.'"[55]

In his *Atiquot* report, Amos Kloner suggests "Jesus, son of Joseph" as a possible reading as well, although he leaves room for some doubt with regard to the reading of that name *Yeshua*.

> "On the narrow side, just below the rim, the name... (Yeshua (?) son of Yehosef' is inscribed."[56]

Additionally, the authors of *The Jesus Family Tomb* claim that the name on the ossuary inscribed in Greek must be read as "Mariamne, also known as *Mara*," and that, further, *Mara* must be translated as 'Master,' 'Teacher,' or 'Apostle.' This interpretation is

---

[54] Simcha Jacobovici and Charles Pellegrino, *The Jesus Family Tomb* (2007) p. 61

[55] *The Lost Tomb of Jesus*, The Discovery Channel (2007)

[56] Amos Kloner, "A Tomb with Inscribed Ossuaries in East Talpiyot, Jerusalem," *Atiquot*, Vol. 29 (1996)

used to link the ossuary that bears the corresponding inscription to the person of Mary Magdalene.

> "The Acts of Philip . . . provided a name . . . for Mary Magdalene: Mariamne; second, it provided a status for Mariamne – she was an apostle, a teacher, or, to use the Aramaic, a 'Mara.'" [57]

> "Inscription specialist Tal Ilan would reveal in December 2005 that part of the second Mary's inscription – 'Mara' – had two possible meanings. It could be read simultaneously as 'Master' and 'Lord.' 'Mara' was preceded by a Greek symbol that means 'also known as.'"[58]

On the website associated with *The Jesus Family Tomb*, a similar claim is made.

> "The ossuary of a Jewish woman who moved in Greek circles. The ossuary of an elite, a "Mara," a "Master." The "Mara" added at the end of her name, in Aramaic, means "Master" or "teacher." It is usually a masculine term, but then, Mariamne was performing duties usually restricted to men on the authority of Jesus. . . . Mariamne, Mary Magdalene, was indeed a Mara."[59]

If these two readings of the ossuaries in question are accepted, they provide a key portion of the foundation of the argument made in the book and documentary. The gospel link between Mary Magdalene and Jesus, son of Joseph, is evident; therefore, these readings and interpretations of the inscriptions are critical to building the foundation for the argument that the tomb is that of Jesus Christ.

Third Claim: The Final Destination of Jesus' Family

In order to buttress the claim that the Talpiot tomb bears, or at one time bore, the remains of Jesus Christ and other members

---

[57] Simcha Jacobovici and Charles Pellegrino, *The Jesus Family Tomb* (2007) p. 102

[58] *Ibid.*, p. 19

[59] "Mariamene e Mara," http://www.jesusfamilytomb.com/the_tomb/mariamene_e_mara.html (2007)

of his family, the book must first establish several points with regard to the history of Jesus' family as well as the relation of their names to the inscriptions found on the ossuaries.

First, the properly interpreted names must be linked to the names that are known to be those of Jesus Christ and his family. Second, it must be demonstrated that all those whose names are inscribed on the tomb's ossuaries must be related. Third, it must be shown for each of the family members that he or she lived in Jerusalem at the time of death or that his or her body was transported to Jerusalem for burial. Each of these claims must be proven in order for the main thesis of the book to be proven.

It is clear from at least two of the canonical gospels that Jesus is identified as the son of Joseph, at least with regard to his assumed paternal lineage. Mary is said to have conceived Jesus by the Holy Ghost while betrothed (but not yet married) to Joseph. After Jesus' birth, Mary and Joseph were married and Joseph became an adoptive father. This would possibly fit with an ossuary inscription read "Jesus, son of Joseph." Given that Jesus was tried and crucified in Jerusalem, it is conceivable that, if he did not ascend bodily into heaven, his bones may have been interred somewhere near the city.

Furthermore, given the assumptions and worldviews of the authors, the ossuary inscribed with *Marya*, or Mary, could possibly be that of Jesus' mother. If so, and assuming she died somewhere near Jerusalem as well, then a link between the ossuary inscribed with *Yeshua bar Yehosef* and the ossuary inscribed with *Marya* becomes plausible.

> "Jesus' mother, Mary, Maria in antiquity, was also of Davidic descent, but, unlike Joseph, according to later Christian tradition, she died in Jerusalem."[60]

The added presence of an ossuary inscribed with the name *Yose*, or a contraction for the name Joseph, further builds the potential of the case. The fate of Joseph, the ostensible human father of Jesus, could possibly had been in Jerusalem, since there is little mention in the Bible of his life beyond his relationship to Mary and no mention of the time or whereabouts of his death. While there is nothing in the biblical literature substantiating the notion that Joseph died in, or that his body was transported to,

---

[60] *The Lost Tomb of Jesus*, The Discovery Channel (2007)

Jerusalem, there is also nothing that explicitly contradicts this possibility. Thus, if several assumptions about Joseph's life and death are made, the possibility of the tomb being that of Jesus and his immediate family is left open.

On the other hand, *Yose* may refer to the brother of Jesus mentioned in Mark 6:3. Only Jesus brother is referred to explicitly in the Gospels as *Yose*; Jesus' father, Joseph, is never referred to in this manner. Since little is said about this brother in the New Testament or elsewhere, the possibility of his death in Jerusalem is conceivable.

> "*Yose*, or Jose in English, was the brother of Jesus. But the Gospels don't tell us much more than that; he disappears after thee brief citations. What happened to *Yose* is a mystery. But if the ossuaries from the Talpiot tomb belong to the Jesus family, then *Yose* has finally been found."[61]

The inscriptions on the other three ossuaries, *Matya* (a contraction for 'Matthew'), *Yehuda bar Yeshua* ("Judah, son of Jesus"), and *Mariamene e Mara* ("Mary, the Master") pose slightly greater difficulties to the thesis.

There is no mention of a Matthew in the Bible with regard to Jesus' immediate family, and thus the precise identity of this person, his relation to the other members of the family, and, therefore, even the identity of the family itself comes into question. An examination of the lineage of Mary reveals a number of instances of the name 'Matthew,' thus leading the authors to the conclusion that the presence of a Matthew in the family tomb of Jesus is not far-fetched. Instead, this addition would be perfectly in line with the biblical genealogy of Jesus.

> "What is known, however, from the genealogy provided in Luke (3:23), is that unlike Joseph, Mary the mother of Jesus had many "Matthews" in her family. Unlike, say, a "Daniel" or a "Jonah", the appearance of a "Matthew" in this family's tomb is consistent with the information provided in the Gospels."[62]

A similar statement is made in the documentary by Tabor.

---

[61] *The Lost Tomb of Jesus*, The Discovery Channel (2007)

[62] "'Matia': Matthew," http://www.jesusfamilytomb.com/the_tomb/matia.html (2007)

> "I don't think it's odd that we would have a Matthew in this tomb at all. In fact, it's sort of one more congruence and fitting together."[63]

That a Matthew, who was related to Jesus in some manner, might have died in Jerusalem is, thus, a conceivable event, according to the reasoning presented in the book, documentary, and other assorted literature.

The inscribed ossuary that ostensibly bore the remains of Judah (or Judas), son of Jesus, also presents a difficulty. There is no mention in the Bible of Jesus having any children, let alone even being married. Nevertheless, as pointed out in the promotional website for *The Jesus Family Tomb*, neither is there any explicit contradiction to this suggestion.

> "Absolutely nothing in the New Testament indicates that Jesus was celibate. He could very well have been married and had children."[64]

This possibility is raised in *The Jesus Family Tomb* by way of reference to the Gospel of Thomas, a Gnostic gospel believed to have been authored in the second century A.D. It is suggested that Jesus had a son, Judah, who was largely kept secret for fear of the Roman authorities who would have been inclined to kill the offspring of anyone who might have claimed kingship over Rome.

> "This strange code would be impossible to break were it not for an ossuary in Talpiot inscribed "Judah son of Jesus." Can it be that the son [took on a different name] in order to protect him [self] from the Roman authorities? Can it be that Jesus' son has been hiding – touchingly, like a child – in plain sight all along?"[65]

Given the secrecy supposed to have surrounded the possible offspring of Jesus, the place of his death becomes a wide-open realm of possibilities that includes Jerusalem. Thus, the presence of the ossuary bearing the name Judah is made to fit with the other names on other ossuaries.

---

[63] *The Lost Tomb of Jesus*, The Discovery Channel (2007)

[64] "Judah, Son of Jesus," http://www.jesusfamilytomb.com/the_tomb/yehuda_bar_yeshua.html (2007)

[65] Simcha Jacobovici and Charles Pellegrino, *The Jesus Family Tomb* (2007) p. 108

The final difficulty for the thesis is the ossuary with the inscription *Mariamene e Mara*. As already noted, this was translated in *The Jesus Family Tomb* as "Mary, the Master" or "Mary, the Teacher." However, one of the major claims presented in the book is that this Mary is actually Mary Magdalene. This claim is central to building up to the conclusion that the Jesus of the Talpiot tomb is the Jesus Christ of the Bible. However substantiated, the claim that *Mariamene* refers to Mary Magdalene would add a further biblical link to the tomb's history, assuming also that the final resting place of Mary Magdalene was in Jerusalem.

Fourth Claim: Mariamene e Mara as Mary Magdalene

In order to complete the connection between the ossuaries found in the Talpiot tomb and the family of Jesus, the authors undertake the task of determining the referent of the inscription *Mariamene e Mara*. Based on the preceding assumption that the translation is "Mary, the Master" or "Mary, the Teacher," reference to the apocryphal book Acts of Philip is made to substantiate the assertion that the Mary inscribed on the ossuary is actually Mary Magdalene.

> "Mariamne is the name by which the Magdalene has been known, as found in such non-canonical works as The Acts of Philip. Prominent Harvard scholars François Bovon and Karen King point out that not only is Mary Magdalene called 'Mariamne' in these texts, Jesus' mother is called 'Maria' – coincidentally the name inscribed on the other 'Mary' ossuary."[66]

The reference to Mary as 'teacher' or 'apostle,' according to the authors, may have been with regard to her position of leadership discussed in Acts of Philip.

> "And what of the 'Mara' added at the end of her name, in Aramaic, means 'Master' or 'teacher.' It is usually a masculine term, but then, Mariamne was performing duties usually restricted to men on the authority of Jesus."[67]

---

[66] "The Theological Mariamene," http://www.jesusfamilytomb.com/the_tomb/mariamene_e_mara/theological_mary.html (2007)

[67] "Mariamene," http://www.jesusfamilytomb.com/the_tomb/mariamene_e_mara/mary_as_master.html (2007)

Additionally, François Bovon, Frothingham Professor of the History of Religion at Harvard Divinity School, is cited with regard to Mary's supposed leadership status in the Christian church.

> "This Mary Magdalene, this Mary from the Acts of Philip, is clearly the equal of the other apostles – and, as depicted, is even more enlightened than Philip."[68]

The documentary also cites Bovon, who apparently suggests that Mary Magdalene's death could have been in Jerusalem: a necessary event if she were to have also been buried there.

> "According to the Acts of Philip, at the end of the story, Mariamne is . . . supposed to go home to Israel to the Jordan Valley, and the author has an allusion that [this is] where she would die and be buried."[69]

The narrator of *The Lost Tomb of Jesus* makes the same statement with greater clarity.

> "The Acts of Philip clearly [tells] us that Mary Magdalene, Jesus' most trusted apostle, dies here in Jerusalem."[70]

With regard to the language of the inscription *Mariamene e Mara*, the authors of *The Jesus Family Tomb* suggest that the use of Greek, rather than Hebrew, may be have been reasonably expected, since Mary Magdalene may have spoken Greek. Bovon is once again cited to this effect.

> "The New Testament's Mary Magdalene began as a wealthy sponsor of the Jesus ministry, originating from his neighborhood near the Sea of Galilee. Now, archaeologists can tell you that this region was very much bilingual. Sepphoris, not very far from Nazareth, was a major Roman-dominated, Greek-speaking city. So I would expect that Mary Magdalene spoke Greek in addition to Hebrew and Aramaic."[71]

---

[68] Simcha Jacobovici and Charles Pellegrino, *The Jesus Family Tomb* (2007) p. 97

[69] *The Lost Tomb of Jesus*, The Discovery Channel (2007)

[70] *The Lost Tomb of Jesus*, The Discovery Channel (2007)

[71] Simcha Jacobovici and Charles Pellegrino, *The Jesus Family Tomb* (2007) p. 101

Since there was no blood relation between Mary Magdalene and Jesus suggested in the Bible, another relationship must be considered if they were to both be interred in the same family tomb. One possible connection is through marriage.

> "The Gospel of Philip is a particularly valuable source of information about Mary Magdalene. From it we glean that Mariamne/Magdalene was sister to Philip (one of the twelve original apostles) and Martha; . . . and that she died at the Jordan River, 'near Jerusalem.' It also reveals the following tantalizing tidbit: 'There were three who always walked with the Lord: Mary, his mother, and her sister, and Magdalene, the one who was called his companion. His sister and his mother and his companion were each a Mary.' This text has led many to surmise a marriage between Jesus and Mary Magdalene."[72]

Based on these claims, which rely heavily on the Gnostic text of the Acts of Philip, believed to have been written in the fourth century A.D.,[73] a place for *Mariamene e Mara* in the tomb of Jesus' family comes into view. The identification of this inscription with Mary Magdalene, along with the possibility of her marriage to Jesus, would, if true, lend further credence to the thesis that the Talpiot tomb is indeed that of Jesus Christ.

Fifth Claim: Statistical Analysis

To buttress the thesis of *The Jesus Family Tomb* with numerical data, the authors sought a statistical analysis of the case. Since the names Jesus, Mary, and Joseph were extremely common in the first century, it is to be expected that they would also be found inscribed in many tombs. Nevertheless, the possibility of finding the names in a given combination is less likely than that of finding any individual name, especially when the number of names involved increases beyond two or three.

This phenomenon may be understood by way of analogy to a deck of cards. Any particular card, such as an ace, has a fairly high probability of being picked at random from a deck. For this

---

[72] "The Historical Mary Magdalene," http://www.jesusfamilytomb.com/the_tomb/mariamene_e_mara/historical_mary.html (2007)

[73] Peter H. Desmond, "Fourth-Century Church Tales," http://www.harvardmagazine.com/on-line/0500113.html (May-June 2000)

example, the odds are one out of thirteen, since there are four aces in a deck of fifty-two cards. However, for a particular hand of cards, say an ace, a king, and a queen, the odds of obtaining that hand decrease almost exponentially. The calculation of the probability is made by multiplying together the odds of each individual event, so that the odds of drawing an ace, a king, and a queen are very nearly 1 out of 13 x 13 x 13, or 1 out of 2197.

Applying this reasoning to the case of the Talpiot tomb, by considering the ratios of people with a given name to the rest of the population in Israel around the time of Jesus, a similar calculation of statistics may be made. The estimated regularity of the name Jesus, son of Joseph, is 1 out of 190, meaning for every 190 people taken at random from Israel in the first century, one was Jesus, who is also the son of Joseph. For Mariamne (or *Mariamene*), the regularity is estimated at 1 out of 160; for Matthew (or *Matya*), 1 out of 40; for Joseph (or *Yose*), 1 out of 20; for Mary (or *Marya*), 1 out of 4. The documentary cites Andrey Feuerverger, professor of statistics at the University of Toronto, with regard to the next step of the calculation.

> "The individual probability factors, even though they're not terribly small in any one particular case, when you multiply them all together, it actually starts to build up a picture that the overall thing that you've seen is actually a very rare event."[74]

If Matthew is eliminated from this calculation, since he is not mentioned in the Gospels as being a relative of Jesus, a more conservative number is obtained. This leads to a statistical estimate of about 1 out of 2,400,000. If this number is multiplied by a factor of 4 to take into consideration any historical biases present in the assumptions, and if the number is also multiplied by 1,000, representing an estimate of the number of tombs from 1st century Jerusalem. The final, conservative estimate is about 1 out of 600. This means that, based on the assumptions given thus far, there is only a 1 out of 600 chance that this is *not* the tomb of Jesus Christ. That is to say, there is a 99.8% chance, given the worldviews and assumptions of the authors, that the Talpiot tomb is that of the historical Jesus.

---

[74] *The Lost Tomb of Jesus*, The Discovery Channel (2007)

> "By the end, [Feuerverger's] model concludes that there is only one chance in six hundred that the Talpiot tomb is not the Jesus family tomb, if Mariamne can be linked to Mary Magdalene."[75]

Thus, based on the calculation here, it would appear that statistical evidence lends credence to the hypothesis of *The Jesus Family Tomb*.

Sixth Claim: DNA Evidence: Mary Magdalene as Jesus' Wife

As mentioned previously, the assumption that Mariamne (who is apparently linked to Mary Magdalene) must be Jesus' wife is a critical factor in proving the hypothesis that the tomb is that of Jesus Christ. Since Mary Magdalene was not said to be related to Jesus by blood, relation by marriage is proposed as the solution that allows for her interment in the same tomb. In order to buttress this claim and to attempt to show that there was no blood relation (a fact that could be devastating to the hypothesis), DNA evidence was examined.

> "All scriptural records – whether canonical or apocryphal – were clear on one genealogical point: Jesus of Nazareth and Mary Magdalene . . . would be two individuals who had no family ties."[76]

After taking samples of biological material (presumed to be bone fragments) from both the Jesus and *Mariamene* ossuaries, DNA analysis was performed at the Paleo-DNA Laboratory at Lakehead University in Thunder Bay, Ontario. The results showed that there was no blood relation between the sources of the samples.

> "In 2005 producer Felix Golubev, working together with scholar Steve Pfann and forensic archaeologist Steven Cox, removed human residue from both the Jesus and Mariamne ossuaries. The tiny fragments were then shipped to Dr. Carney Matheson of the Paleo-DNA Lab at Lakehead University in Ontario. Dr. Matheson and his team were not able to extract nuclear DNA from the degraded samples. However, they were able to extract mitochondrial DNA from both the Jesus and Mariamne ossuaries. This allowed them to confirm

---

[75] *Ibid.*

[76] Simcha Jacobovici and Charles Pellegrino, *The Jesus Family Tomb* (2007) p. 168

> that these were indeed Middle Eastern people of antiquity and that they were *not* related."[77]

Since the DNA extracted from the samples was mitochondrial rather than nuclear, and since mitochondrial DNA is only passed down genetically in women, the results of the DNA test could only show maternal relationship.

> "[Mitochondrial DNA is] the DNA inherited *maternally*, from mother to child. This means that we can identify maternal relationships. Meaning, we can only address questions such as: 'Are these two individuals – one male and the other female – mother and child? Are they brother and sister? Or are they two unrelated individuals?'"[78]

Nevertheless, the lack of blood relation led the authors to conclude that the relationship between Jesus and Mariamne, since they were interred in the same family tomb, must have been marriage.

> "[We can then conclude] that this man and woman do not share the same mother. They cannot be mother and child. They cannot, maternally, be brother and sister. And so, for these particular samples, because they come from the same tomb – and we suspect it to be a familial tomb – these two individuals, if they were unrelated, would most likely have been husband and wife."[79]

To prevent bias on the part of those conducting the DNA analysis, the samples provided were identified only by the reference numbers of the ossuaries: 80-500 and 80-503.[80] Additionally, it was only mentioned that the samples "had come from an ancient Jerusalem tomb" and that the task of interest was to "reconstruct the family relationships of a royal lineage."[81]

In light of the results of the DNA analysis and the conclusion that the Jesus and Mariamne of the tomb were related by marriage, the narrator of *The Lost Tomb of Jesus* connects this conclusion to various biblical texts.

> "Mary Magdalene appears with more frequency than other women in the

---

[77] *Ibid.*, p. 206-207

[78] *Ibid.*, p. 170

[79] *Ibid.*, p. 172

[80] Amos Kloner, "A Tomb with Inscribed Ossuaries in East Talpiyot, Jerusalem," *Atiquot*, Vol. 29 (1996)

[81] Simcha Jacobovici and Charles Pellegrino, *The Jesus Family Tomb* (2007) p. 168

> canonical gospels, always a close follower of Jesus. The presence at the crucifixion is consistent with the role of a grieving wife and widow. And, so, perhaps Jesus and Mary Magdalene were married, as the DNA results from the Talpiot ossuaries suggest. And perhaps their union was kept secret to protect a potential dynasty."[82]

Thus, in addition to those places where Mary Magdalene was referred to in the Bible as a "close follower of Jesus," the fact that the biblical narrative (and many other texts) fail to mention any further relationship becomes added evidence due to the potential threat to both Mary Magdalene and any offspring.

Seventh Claim: The James Ossuary

Near the end of 2002, the existence of an ossuary inscribed with the words *Ya'akov bar Yehosef akhui di Yeshua* ("James, son of Joseph, brother of Jesus") was made public in *Biblical Archaeological Review*. The Aramaic inscription was strikingly similar to the name of the biblical figure of James, who was both son of Joseph and brother of Jesus Christ. The owner of the tomb, a private Israeli collector named Oded Golan, claimed to have purchased the ossuary from an Arab antiquities dealer in Jerusalem.[83]

In a seemingly unrelated situation, according to Shimon Gibson, one of the archaeologists who first examined the tomb after its discovery in 1980, one of the ten Talpiot ossuaries had gone missing according to Israel Antiquities Authority (IAA) records.

> "I went to the storerooms of the Israel Antiquities Authority in Bet Shemesh. They provided me with this computer [printout] which indicates that from this tomb there are nine items. . . . And it has the description of these ossuaries and where they are located in the storerooms."[84]

If these two events were connected, however, and the missing ossuary was the same as the James ossuary from the collection of Golan, another piece of evidence would be added to the case, further suggesting that the Talpiot tomb was, indeed, that of Jesus Christ.

---

[82] *The Lost Tomb of Jesus*, The Discovery Channel (2007)

[83] *Ibid.*

[84] *Ibid.*

Chapter Three: Fundamental Claims

> "The numerous accounts of James' life show an early Christian of such importance that if it was at all possible, he would most certainly have been laid beside Jesus in death."[85]

In order to buttress the claim that the missing Talpiot ossuary and the James ossuary were, in fact, the same, several steps were taken. One test involved comparison of the dimensions of the ossuary as cataloged in the IAA records with the dimensions of the James ossuary. The measurements indicated a match, as attested by Tabor in *The Lost Tomb of Jesus*.

> "I checked the dimensions... the dimensions of [the missing] ossuary are the same as the James ossuary."[86]

In spite of this match, the indictment of Oded Golan and others in 2004 for antiquities fraud with regard to the James ossuary and other artifacts has brought any relationship with the Talpiot tomb into question.

> "In February 2003, the Israel Antiquities Authority confiscated [the James ossuary] and appointed a team of 15 epigraphers and physical scientists to analyze and judge the authenticity of the inscription. In June 2003 the IAA declared the ossuary itself to be genuine, but the inscription was a partial forgery. A month later Oded Golan was arrested on suspicion of faking antiquities."[87]

Although the portion of the inscription *akhui di Yeshua* ("brother of Jesus") was determined to be a forgery added by Golan or his accomplices, the remainder was deemed genuine.

> "A lot of people have concluded – experts – that the James ossuary is a forgery, but nobody says it's all a forgery. And the position now of the Israel Antiquities Authority is that it originally said 'James, son of Joseph.'"[88]

Since the origin of the ossuary had been brought into question by fraudulent activities, the next step in determining

---

[85] *Ibid.*

[86] *Ibid.*

[87] Laurence Gardner, "The Jesus Ossuary" (March 2007) p. 7-8

[88] *The Lost Tomb of Jesus*, The Discovery Channel (2007)

whether it was from the Talpiot tomb was examination of the *patina*, or the chemical 'fingerprint' of deposits that collect over years on surfaces, of the ossuary.

> "In theory, the patina inside a tomb or on the surfaces of its artifacts should develop its own chemically distinct signature, depending on a constellation of variable conditions, including the minerals and bacterial populations present at any specific location and the quantities of water moving through that specific 'constellation.' If such a chemical 'fingerprint' existed, scanning patina samples on a quantum level with an electron microprobe would reveal a chemical spectrum that could be matched to a specific tomb and to any objects that come from it."[89]

Thus, by examining the patina of the James ossuary and comparing it to the patina of other ossuaries known to have originated from the Talpiot tomb, a strong connection between them could either be established or discounted.

> "If the James patina matches the ossuaries from the Talpiot tomb, it will be strong evidence that the James ossuary is the missing bone box and belongs to the family of Jesus."[90]

In order to further establish a match between the James ossuary and the Talpiot tomb by way of patina 'fingerprinting,' random samples from other locations were also collected and compared. By showing the lack of a match between the James patina and other random patina samples, the evidentiary value of a match between the James patina and other Talpiot tomb patinas becomes much greater.

> "The patina samples from the Talpiot tomb match with the James ossuary. But what about the random samples? As it turns out, none of them match Talpiot. The same [patina signature] as that of the Talpiot tomb are exhibited only by the James patina. This is key evidence indicating the ossuary inscribed 'James, son of Joseph, brother of Jesus' is the missing ossuary from the Talpiot tomb."[91]

Thus, based on this evidence, not only is the origin of an apparently stolen ossuary discovered, but a further link with biblical names and history is also established. It would appear that this

---

[89] Simcha Jacobovici and Charles Pellegrino, *The Jesus Family Tomb* (2007) p. 176

[90] *The Lost Tomb of Jesus*, The Discovery Channel (2007)

[91] *Ibid.*

further supports the hypothesis that the Talpiot tomb is in fact the tomb of Jesus Christ.

Eighth Claim: Reliability of the New Testament Texts

In order for any of the assumptions and claims about the Talpiot ossuaries to be true with regard to Jesus Christ, a vast portion of the New Testament must be shown to be false. Since there are so many references in the canonical gospels, epistles, and Revelation of John to Jesus Christ's resurrection from the dead, bodily ascension into heaven, and eternal life with God, the discovery of a tomb that bears his remains is not compatible with the truthfulness of these texts. In the foreword to *The Jesus Family Tomb*, James Cameron introduces the general tone of suspicion, which permeates the entire book, with regard to the veracity of the New Testament texts.

> "The Gospels as we know them today have been retranscribed and rewritten many times and translated from one language to another – from Aramaic to Greek to Coptic to Latin to various forms of English – with corresponding losses in nuanced meaning. They have been edited by Church fathers, centuries after the original words were spoken, to conform to their subsequent vision of orthodoxy. And yet, in the absence of the tiniest scrap of concrete physical evidence, they were our only record of the life and times of Jesus."[92]

Furthermore, also in the pages of the book, the authors cite the discussion in the Gospel of Matthew regarding a rumor circulating in Jerusalem around the time of Jesus' crucifixion. It is suggested that, although Matthew denied this rumor, it was actually true: the body of Jesus, far from being resurrected, had been spirited away by his disciples.

> "But the Gospels also hint at an alternative explanation for Jesus' empty tomb. Matthew says there was another story circulating in Jerusalem after the Crucifixion of Jesus. Although Matthew calls it a lie, according to the rumor, [Jesus'] disciples secretly came by night and stole away with their Master's body. . . . If the disciples took the body, there is only one thing they could have done with it. They would have reburied it . . . and then stored his bones in an ossuary, sealed away forever deep in the recesses of his family tomb."[93]

---

[92] Simcha Jacobovici and Charles Pellegrino, *The Jesus Family Tomb* (2007) p. x

[93] *Ibid.*, p. 2-3

For the quest to identify the ossuaries and remains found in the tomb with Jesus Christ and his family, this is perhaps the most fundamental premise: two millennia's worth of history, culture, and testimony must be discarded as being largely based on a lie. Although the documentary, *The Lost Tomb of Jesus*, does cite a professed Christian, professor emeritus John Dominic Crossan of DePaul University, with regard to the lack of impact that the discovery of Jesus' tomb might have on his faith, this can hardly be considered an orthodox Christian position in line with the New Testament text.

> "If the bones of Jesus were to be found in an ossuary in Jerusalem tomorrow – without doubt let's say they are definitely agreed to be the bones of Jesus – would that destroy Christian faith? It certainly would not destroy my Christian faith. I leave what happens to bodies up to God."[94]

The narrator makes clear the position of the documentary, albeit in noncommittal language.

> "It seems that Christians can accept the possibility that the remains of Jesus were transferred to a family tomb. Thereafter, he could have risen and appeared to his followers as the Gospels report. According to Christian faith, Jesus then ascended to heaven. In theory, the ascension could have been spiritual, leaving his body behind. In fact, those who take a strictly historical approach to the Gospels would expect to find Jesus' remains in his family tomb."[95]

Jesus Christ: Dead or Alive?

Simcha Jacobovici, Charles Pellegrino, James Cameron, and James Tabor, in claiming that Jesus Christ's remains have been found, stand squarely against the words of the Apostle Paul. Against 2,000 years of world history that has seen the slow, but steady, growth of the Christian Church, these four men have made claims and sought to show that, unlike the innumerable preceding scholars who have investigated and debated the person and status of Jesus Christ, they have found the truth. The remainder of this discussion shall address the very question with regard to the claim that the Talpiot tomb is that of Jesus Christ: Is it fact or fiction?

> "Now if Christ is preached that He has been raised from the dead, how do

---

[94] *The Lost Tomb of Jesus*, The Discovery Channel (2007)
[95] *Ibid.*

> some among you say that there is no resurrection of the dead? But if there is no resurrection of the dead, then Christ is not risen. And if Christ is not risen, then our preaching is empty and your faith is also empty. Yes, and we are found false witnesses of God, because we have testified of God that He raised up Christ, whom He did not raise up – if in fact the dead do not rise. For if the dead do not rise, then Christ is not risen. And if Christ is not risen, your faith is futile; you are still in your sins! Then also those who have fallen asleep in Christ have perished. If in this life only we have hope in Christ, we are of all men the most pitiable."[96]

---

[96] 1 Corinthians 15:12-19 (NKJV)

Talpiot Tomb Entrance 1980

(Source: PR Newswire)

Chapter Three: Fundamental Claims

STUDY QUESTIONS:

1. Though there were other claims and ideas in the documentary, why are these eight claims the most important?

first claim: an unreported discovery

"The Jesus Tomb: Excavated But 'Unknown' for 27 Years"
-Simcha Jacobovici

On Wednesday, April 3, 1996, James D. Tabor posted a question in an Internet discussion forum regarding the possibility of the Talpiot tomb belonging to Jesus and His family. The forum, attended by scholars and archaeologists, was hosted by the Orion Center of Hebrew University in Jerusalem and was created for the purpose of discussing the Dead Sea Scrolls and associated literature.

> "I sure many of you have seen the AP and Reuters stories that circulated today — at first I thought it was just an April Fools Day prank but in checking a bit it seems the basic story is solid – i.e., the facts as reported below. Although we all know the names mentioned are common, it does seem that their presence in a single site should have been at least publicized and discussed when they were discovered in 1980. It is also interesting to see all the clerics rushing to assure everyone that this could not be that family. I think Joseph Zias, who probably knows the most about this, is out of the country (Israel I mean), but perhaps we can get a report from him upon his return. Any comments in the meantime?"[97]

Following Tabor's post, a series of exchanges began, culminating in a rebuke from scholars like Drs. Dale M. Cannon,

---

[97] James D. Tabor, Discussion thread, http://orion.huji.ac.il/orion/archives/1996a/msg00145.html (April 3, 1996)

Chapter Four: 1st claim – An Unreported Discovery

Kevin D. Johnson, and Niels Peter Lemche. Johnson reviewed the evidence and dismissed Tabor's suggestion as both out of place in the Orion Center discussion thread as well as ludicrous in its own right.

> "I cannot believe that such a ridiculous story has made it in such a scholarly list. . . . I regularly lurk on this list, but I have just got to say that this whole topic is utterly stupid."[98]

Tabor, after being chastened by his colleagues, discontinued his pursuit of the subject in the Orion Center forum.

> "Since several had complained that this Jerusalem ossuary name discussion was out of place on the Orion List, having little or nothing to do with [the Dead Sea Scrolls], I have dropped it--duly chastened." [99]

Based on this exchange, the clearest fact is that Tabor, if no one else, knew quite well that that the Talpiot tomb existed and that it contained ossuaries with names of biblical note. More than a decade passed between this Internet discussion and the publishing of *The Jesus Family Tomb*, leaving Tabor with no excuse for not having himself publicized the matter further. In spite of the rejection of the topic in the Orion Center forum, there were, no doubt, plenty of other outlets for discussing the matter publicly. The news media has shown itself to be a very willing accessory to publication of sensationalistic stories, whether or not they might offend orthodox Christians. The Talpiot tomb discovery is no exception.

The world press published a number of speculative claims about the Talpiot tomb in 1996, leading ultimately, in the same year, to Amos Kloner's republication in *Atiquot* of the findings regarding the tomb. Popular material that discussed the tomb and its contents included the *Sunday Times* article "The Tomb That Dare Not Speak Its Name" in the United Kingdom as well as "The Body in Question," a television documentary in the *Heart of the Matter* series on BBC. Further reporting took place in *USA Today* and *The Irish Times*.

---

[98] Kevin D. Johnson, Discussion thread,
http://orion.huji.ac.il/orion/archives/1996a/msg00160.html (April 3, 1996)

[99] James D. Tabor, Discussion thread,
http://orion.mscc.huji.ac.il/orion/archives/1996a/msg00219.html (April 8, 1996)

Additionally, at least one book, the 2003 *Excavating Jesus* by Jonathan L. Reed and John Dominic Crossan, also mentioned the matter, along with, in the same year, a Michael S. Heiser paper and presentation devoted to debunking the notion that the Talpiot tomb was that of Jesus Christ and his family.

Reed, a Professor of Religion at the University of La Verne in California and no friend of orthodox Christianity, made a statement in response to the notion that the Talpiot tomb had gone unreported.

> "I wrote about these ossuaries on pages 19-20 of the revised edition of Dom Crossan's and my *Excavating Jesus* . . . and dismiss them as coincidental. My letter to the [Society of Biblical Literature] Forum attacks [*The Lost Tomb of Jesus*], which, along with [*The Jesus Family Tomb*], the producers' statements at the press conference and in subsequent interviews, make the misleading claim that no one ever thought through the issue. The Talpiot ossuaries were allegedly forgotten and buried deep inside the bowels of the [Israel Antiquities Authority]. My point is that all serious scholars who know about ossuaries knew about this discovery. Many scholars had read Kloner's report and [Rahmani's] catalogue. Why is there no lengthy bibliography? No one, including fine New Testament scholars like Evans and McCane, thought that denying the tomb's connection to Jesus of Nazareth merited a serious, in-depth article. Based on the inscriptions, the use [of] statistics, the DNA, and the patina analysis, in short, every bit of evidence that the documentary and book produce, I still do not think a lengthy article is warranted." [100]

Heiser has pointed out the conspiratorial atmosphere portrayed by Jacobovici in *The Jesus Family Tomb*, especially with regard to archaeologists Amos Kloner and Shimon Gibson.

> "One of the questions that immediately surfaces is, 'Why didn't anyone think this was earth-shattering news before now?' In his book, Jacobovici answers this question with a mildly conspiratorial air. He repeatedly casts Amos Kloner as a man struggling against the knowledge that he had stumbled into salvaging the tomb of Jesus of Nazareth but who bravely decided to suppress that truth. . . . Gibson fares somewhat less favorably, coming across as a professional more interested in keeping his job than . . . saying what he thought. . . . There are two primary obstacles to acceptance of Jacobovici's thesis for Kloner and a panoply of other scholars: the commonality of the names and the identification of one of the ossuaries as that of Mary Magdalene. The hesitance is not driven by a willful suppression of self-evident truth, but by the desire for coherent, factual evidence." [101]

---

[100] Jonathan L. Reed, "In Response to Tabor," http://www.sbl-site.org/Article.aspx?ArticleId=657

[101] Michael S. Heiser, "Evidence Real and Imagined: Thinking Clearly About the 'Jesus Family Tomb,'" http://www.michaelsheiser.com/Jesus%20Tomb%20article%20Heiser.pdf

In 2007 James D. Tabor, along with James Cameron, Simcha Jacobovici, and Charles Pellegrino, announced to the world that they had found the tomb of Jesus of Nazareth and that this tomb had fallen through the "archaeological cracks." Jacobovici was confident enough to name one of his promotional interviews "The Jesus Tomb: Excavated But Unknown for 27 Years." This claim was made in the face of numerous references to the Talpiot tomb (many of which are discussed in Chapter 2) in both popular and scholarly publications.

There are only two possible explanations for the protrayal of the book and documentary as news or as first looks into an otherwise ignored discovery. Given that so much material has discussed the find publicly, much of it having been available for at least a decade before the release of the book and documentary, the writers and producers must have ignored past publications either out of a lack of having performed sufficient background investigation, thus bringing their scholarly credentials into question, or out of a willful ignorance, thus bringing their motives and tactics into question.

Given that Tabor had known about the tomb for at least a decade, and that he was an often-cited consultant, ignorance out of a lack of sufficient research is not a plausible excuse. Tabor would have been expected to have mentioned past discussions of the topic because of his own personal experience, if nothing else.

Conclusion

The only rational conclusion is that Tabor, Jacobovici, Pellegrino, and Cameron knew very well that the Talpiot tomb had been discussed in both popular and scholarly outlets. Whatever the motivation, be it greed, deception, personal animosity, or simply a desire to create a more compelling story, *The Jesus Family Tomb* and *The Lost Tomb of Jesus* were presented to either downplay or ignore the past discussion of the topic in question. Only by doing this could a rehash of "old news" be trumpeted as a groundbreaking discovery.

There were far too many other stories and reports about this tomb to dismiss by simply saying that the discovery in 1980 went 'ignored,' that no one "[took] notice," that it "wasn't really talked about," that "most scholars had no idea [it] existed," or that it had "fallen bewteen the archaeological cracks." This language exudes with a sense of intrigue, but it cannot stand up to even a cursory glance through the history of the tomb. The discussions of the find in scholarly forums alone, not to mention popular publications, are too numerous to dismiss.

As mentioned previously, whether the tomb had been discussed prior to the 2007 release of *The Jesus Family Tomb* is not relevant to whether the ossuaries truly bore the bones of Jesus Christ and his family. Nevertheless, that the claim made by the authors in this case has been so soundly refuted suggests that the rest of the claims made must be scrutinized with added suspicion and that the biases of those who wrote the story may be showing forth with undue bluntness.

Chapter Four: 1st claim – An Unreported Discovery

STUDY QUESTIONS:

1. When did Dr. James Tabor explore the idea that the Talpiot tomb was the final resting place of Jesus of Nazareth?

2. Name some plausible reasons why the authors failed to mention the fact that *USA Today* and other newspapers have reported the Talpiot tomb in the past.

3. How important is it for a film's ratings or book sales to purport that it is revealing a "new" discovery?

5

second claim: inscriptions

"If that doesn't say 'Jesus son of Joseph,' yes, it all falls apart."
-Simcha Jacobovici

Proper reading and interpretation of the inscriptions on the Talpiot ossuaries are critical to the thesis posed in *The Jesus Family Tomb*. If the markings on one or more of the ossuaries have been misread, whether due to physical damage or erosion of the surfaces, personal bias on the part of those investigating the tomb, or fraudulent alteration of the inscriptions, or if there has been misinterpretation of the inscriptions, the entire case becomes suspect.

With regard to the inscription *Yeshua bar Yehosef*, were it to be shown that this rendering was based on a misreading of the markings on the ossuary, the entire thesis of the book and documentary would fall apart. In the case of *Mariamene e Mara*, although proof that this did not refer to Mary Magdalene would be extremely detrimental to the notion that the tomb was that of Jesus Christ, it would not necessarily topple the case.

Regardless of the consequences, cross-examination of the reading and interpretation of the two controversial inscriptions must be pursued.

Yeshua: A Properly Read Inscription?

In *The Jesus Family Tomb*, the difficulty in reading the inscription is acknowledged with regard to the ossuary that is claimed to be that of Jesus Christ. Levy Yitzhak Rahmani, whose 1994 publication *Catalogue of Jewish Ossuaries: In the Collections of the State of Israel* specifically lists the Talpiot ossuaries, and Frank

Moore Cross, professor emeritus at Harvard Divinity School, are mentioned in support of the reading *Yeshua bar Yehosef*.

> "Of all the inscriptions found in the Talpiot tomb, the 'Jesus, son of Joseph' is the hardest to read. That's also a fact. It's not that deciphering it is controversial; everyone, from the noted epigrapher L. Y. Rahmani to the legendary Frank Moore Cross of Harvard, agrees that the inscription on the ossuary must be read 'Jesus, son of Joseph' and no other way. But the fact remains that the inscription is written in such a fast and cursive hand that it is, in a sense, hiding in plain sight." [102]

Despite the authors' pronouncement to the contrary, there is considerable disagreement over the inscription. Dr. Rochelle I. S. Altman, a scholar with special interest in ancient phonetic writing systems, is one such dissenter. Altman authored a report identifying the James ossuary as a partial forgery,[103] and recently commented in an e-mail correspondence about the divergence of opinion on the reading of the *Yeshua* ossuary.

> "Rahmani put a question mark on the possible name. Further, Rahmani could not have made it [any] clearer that this was only a *possible* reading. And, as noted, [Dr. Stephen J.] Pfann thinks [the correct reading] may be *Hanan*." [104]

Indeed, in Rahmani's 1994 publication, he mentions the difficulty associated with reading the inscription on the supposed Jesus ossuary and suggests *Yeshua* as a possible reading based, in part, on the more clearly inscribed *Yehuda bar Yeshua* ossuary.

> "Yeshua'(?), son of Yehosef ... The first name, preceded by a large cross-mark, is difficult to read, as the incisions are clumsily carved and badly scratched." [105]

Amos Kloner also makes note of the difficulty in reading the inscription in his 1996 report published in *Atiquot*.

> "On the narrow side, just below the rim, the name ... (Yeshua (?) son of Yehosef) is inscribed. ... It is preceded by an X. ... The first name following the X mark is difficult to read. In contrast to other ossuaries in this tomb, the

---

[102] Simcha Jacobovici and Charles Pellegrino, *The Jesus Family Tomb* (2007) p. 194-195

[103] Rochelle I. Altman, "Official Report on the James Ossuary," http://www.bibleinterp.com/articles/Official_Report.htm

[104] E-mail correspondence, (March 11, 2007)

[105] L.Y. Rahmani, *A Catalogue of Jewish Ossuaries: In the Collections of the State of Israel* (1994)

[106] Amos Kloner, "A Tomb with Inscribed Ossuaries in East Talpiyot, Jerusalem," *Atiquot*, Vol. 29 (1996)

The Jesus Tomb: Is It Fact or Fiction? Scholars Chime In

> incisions are here superficial and cursorily carved." [106]

Stephen J. Pfann, an expert in Semitic languages and president of the University of the Holy Land in Jerusalem, also suggested that the inscription may not be *Yeshua*, but some other name instead.

> "I don't think it says Yehoshua. It says Hanun or something." [107]

Furthermore, in an e-mail correspondence, Pfann further discussed his view of the inscription.

> "The 'Jesus' inscription is indeed two names one superimposed over the other. I'm working on it. . . . I see a different name underneath." [108]

In a recorded interview, Pfann suggests that the name of another family member may have been written over a previous name, thus resulting in the difficulty reading the *Yeshua* portion of the inscription. His reasoning rests primarily on his observation that the markings read as *Yeshua* were written with a different instrument than that used to create the other portion of the inscription.

> "The name Jesus, Yeshua, is full of scratches, and the lettering that is key to being read as Yeshua is made with a different instrument than the rest of the inscription. Now, I'm not saying that it's necessary that someone in modern times went in and doctored this inscription. It may be more likely that someone in antiquity, when another member of the family was added, in this case it was Yeshua instead of Hanun or . . . Yehuda or whatever else is lying underneath, that they went ahead and re-inscribed that first name for this next one that came in." [109]

Additionally, Steve Caruso, a professional translator at Aramaic Designs and a decade-long student of the Aramaic language with a focus on various forms of Aramaic calligraphy, researched the inscription by way of photographs from the Israel Antiquities Authority (IAA). Using computer graphics to separate each word, Caruso came to the conclusion that *Yeshua* is only *one possible* reading of the inscription. In agreement with the scholars

---

[107] Mati Milstein, "Jesus' Tomb Claim Slammed By Scholars," *National Geographic News*, http://news.nationalgeographic.com/news/2007/02/070228-jesus-tomb.html (February 28, 2007)

[108] E-mail correspondence (March 17, 2007)

[109] Stephen J. Pfann, Interview on Bible.org Radio (March 16, 2007)

cited here, Caruso suggested in an e-mail correspondence that the reading of *Yeshua* is inconclusive.

> "It's possible to read it as 'Jesus, son of Joseph,' but [it is] overall inconclusive. The handwriting is simply too messy and the carving too worn to make a definitive judgment." [110]

In addition to the names mentioned here thus far, other scholars have disputed the accuracy of the claim that the inscription reads *Yeshua*. Although it may be admitted that this is a possible reading, the matter is not as clear as may have been suggested in *The Jesus Family Tomb* and *The Lost Tomb of Jesus*. Israeli epigrapher and professor emeritus Joseph Naveh is one scholar that takes a more cautious position with regard to the reading of the inscription.

> "The 'Joseph' is unmistakable. The 'son of' is okay. And you can certainly read it as 'Jesus,' [but] just not definitely. There are lots of additional lines here that don't belong." [111]

Also taking a moderate approach to the matter is Emile Puech, a professor at the French Biblical and Archaeological School in East Jerusalem.

> "The 'Joseph' is clear. The 'son of' is no problem. The 'Jesus?' It's certainly possible to read it that way." [112]

A third prominent scholar, Ada Yardeni, who has published such books as *The Book of Hebrew Script: History, Palaeography, Script Styles, Calligraphy & Design*, made a similar statement.

> "'Son of Joseph' for sure. The first name? Well, there are lots of markings here, but, yes, it could well be read Jesus." [113]

Clearly, then, there is doubt with regard to the reading of the *Yeshua* inscription, although the possibility that this is a proper reading is left open. The origin and, perhaps, purpose of the other

---

[110] E-mail correspondence (March 3, 2007)

[111] David Horovitz, "Giving 'Jesus' the silent treatment," *Jerusalem Post* (March 1, 2007)

[112] *Ibid.*

[113] *Ibid.*

marks in the inscription must be considered before a final judgment on the matter can be made. To simply dismiss, without evidence, the markings that do not fit in with the reading *Yeshua* as purely unintentional marks or scratches is to make an unwarranted conjecture. Such an approach would show that the hypothesis, far from being open to refutation by evidence, is in fact a preconceived opinion that is held up for rationalization.

Mariamene e Mara: Mary the Master?

The previously mentioned Steven J. Pfann, who questions the reading *Yeshua* from the ostensible Jesus ossuary, also questions the reading of *Mariamene e Mara*, both with regard to its Greek form and its corresponding English translation. Much of the case made in *The Lost Tomb of Jesus* and *The Jesus Family Tomb* depends on a connection between the Greek-inscribed ossuary and the biblical figure of Mary Magdalene. If errors have been made in reading or translating the inscription, what remains of the Talpiot discovery, even barring any misreading of the *Yeshua* ossuary, is simply a family tomb with a collection of names that were exceedingly common in first century Israel.

Pfann suggests that the Greek text must actually be read *Mariame kai Mara*, not *Mariamene e Mara*. Then, in concurrence with Amos Kloner, *Mara* must be read as a contraction of Martha, a common name in first century Israel.

> "Mara, a contraction of Martha, is used here as a second name. This name too is common in the Jewish feminine onomasticon." [114]

According to Pfann, the name *Mariame* was a common and standard Greek form of the Hebrew name *Miriam*.

> "The word as it stands forms 'MARIAME,' which is the normal Greek form of the Hebrew name 'Miriam.'" [115]

Furthermore, based on comparison with other examples of written Greek from contemporaneous texts and based on recognition that the markings were inscribed by two different

---

[114] Amos Kloner, "A Tomb with Inscribed Ossuaries in East Talpiyot, Jerusalem," *Atiquot*, Vol. 29 (1996)

[115] Stephen J. Pfann,"Mary Magdalene is Now Missing: A Corrected Reading of Rahmani Ossuary 701" http://www.uhl.ac/MariameAndMartha.pdf

writers, Pfann suggests that the words *kai Mara* are inscribed in the unique writing of a scribe other than the one who wrote the name *Mariame*.

> "The overall appearance of cursive writing is that there is a graceful sequence of looping strokes as can be seen in KAI MARA. This stands in contrast to the triangular, squared and rather jagged succession strokes of the more formal script used by the first scribe while inscribing MARIAME." [116]

The result, *Mariame kai Mara*, is translated as "Mariam and Mara," or, roughly, "Mary and Martha." The commonality of both these names in first century Israel suggests that their appearance together on an ossuary is altogether unremarkable, as many ossuaries were used for the bones of more than one individual.

> "Due to the fact that (1) an ossuary would often contain more than one individual's bones and (2) these two names are among the most common personal names of the first century, the combination of these two names together on an ossuary is not unique." [117]

Given the unremarkable nature of the ossuary, along with the common names inscribed upon it, attempts to relate the ossuary or its contents to Mary Magdalene become unconvincing.

Richard Bauckham, Professor of New Testament Studies at the University of St. Andrews in Scotland, is another scholar who concurs with Pfann's interpretation of *Mara*. Although he has a different perspective on the writing preceding *Mara*, of fundamental importance is that he agrees both that the inscription refers to two separate people rather than one and that translation of *Mara* as 'master' or 'teacher' is unwarranted.

> "The inscription also has a second name Mara. When Rahmani published this inscription in his catalogue of ossuaries he conjectured that the Greek particle 'e' (meaning 'or') should be supplied between the two names, making them alternative names for the same woman. The 'e' is not actually in the inscription, nor is there space for it between the two names. It is better to suppose that the bones of two women (or perhaps a woman and her child, the diminutive Mariamenon being used for the latter) were placed in the same ossuary (this would not be ... unusual). The name Mara is known to have been used as an abbreviation of the name Martha. The programme makers take it to be the Aramaic word for 'master,' but this is implausible in the context. Beside the

---

[116] *Ibid.*

[117] *Ibid.*

> name Mariamenou on an ossuary, one would expect Mara to be a name, and since it is attested as a name this is the obviously correct reading." [118]

Ben Witherington, Professor of New Testament Interpretation at Asbury Theological Seminary in Kentucky, agreed with the opinion of Bauckham.

> "I concur with this conclusion having now looked closely at the inscription on this particular ossuary. There is no word 'or' in the inscription, in fact there is a slash line separating the first name from the name Mara indicating we are most likely dealing with two different people. Prof. Bauckham has suggested to me that since these are all attested and some are very common Jewish names, that it is more probable this is a Jewish tomb but with no connection to Jesus of Nazareth. This may be so." [119]

Conclusion

Based on the statements of scholars given here, it can in no wise be taken for granted that the inscriptions are to be read as *Yeshua* or *Mariamene e Mara*, as required by the hypothesis of *The Jesus Family Tomb* and *The Lost Tomb of Jesus*. Although these may be possible readings, they are not beyond doubt. Even given the readings as claimed in defense of the hypothesis, there is little evidence to make the rather grand leap to identification of the names with Jesus Christ and Mary Magdalene. To these matters the discussion shall now turn.

---

[118] Richard Bauckham, "Addendum from Prof. Richard Bauckham,"
http://benwitherington.blogspot.com/2007/02/problems-multiple-for-jesus-tomb-theory.html
(February 28, 2007)

[119] Ben Witherington, "Problems multiply for the Jesus tomb theory,"
http://benwitherington.blogspot.com/2007/02/problems-multiple-for-jesus-tomb-theory.html
(February 28, 2007)

Chapter Five: 2nd claim – Inscriptions

ישוע בר יהוסף Yeshua'(?), son of Yehosef
Bibl. ḤA 76, 1981:24-25.
Comm. 1. See Comm. 701:1.
2. The first name, preceded by a large cross-mark, is difficult to read, as the incisions are clumsily carved and badly scratched. There seems to be a vertical stroke representing a *yod*, followed by a *shin*; the *vav* merges with the right stroke of the *'ayin*. The reading ישוע is corroborated by the inscription on No. 702 referring to Yeshua', the father of Yehuda. For the name, see Comm. 9:1.
3. יהוסף: For the name, see Comm. 9:2.

Yeshua inscription with question mark
(Source: Copyright © L.Y. Rahmani)

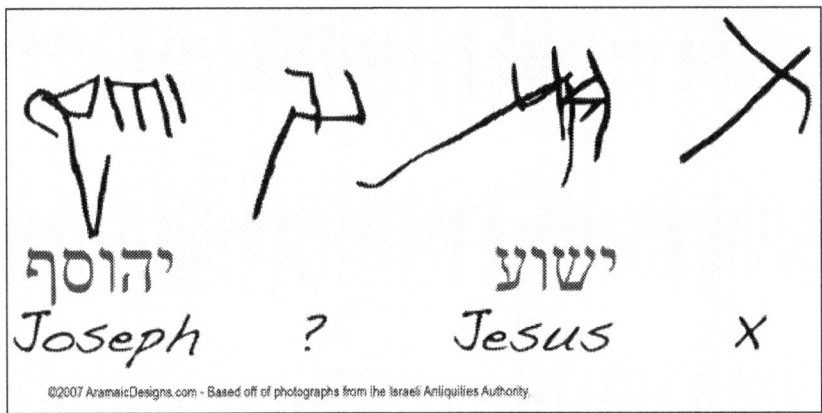

Yeshua bar Joseph
(Source: Copyright © 2007 Aramaic Designs)

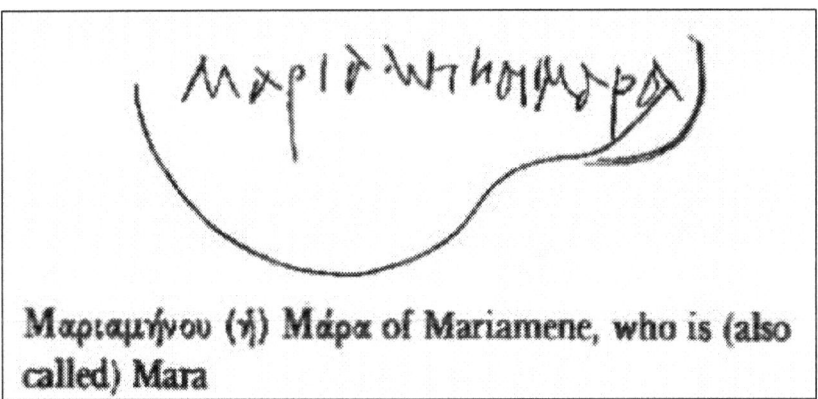

Mariamene inscription
(Source: Copyright © L.Y. Rahmani)

Chapter Five: 2nd claim – Inscriptions

STUDY QUESTIONS:

1. Name the possible reasons why the name "Jesus" was made with a different instrument than the rest of the inscription ("son of Joseph").

2. Name the possible reasons why there seems to be a second name beneath the "Jesus" inscription, as if it was scratched out.

3. How important is it forensically that the tomb was looted and/or vandalized in the past before it was discovered in 1980?

third claim: Jesus family burial in Jerusalem

"In Galilee they might have had such a family burial site, not Judea."
- Dr. Paul L. Maier
Western Michigan University

As discussed in Chapter 3, there are several evidentiary hurdles that must be overcome before the hypothesis that the Talpiot tomb is that of Jesus and his family can be proven. The names found on the ossuaries must be related to the names found in the Bible story, those who bore those names must be shown to have been related accordingly, and each of these people must be proven to have died in or near Jerusalem, leading to subsequent burial in the city.

The authors of *The Jesus Family Tomb* present statements and evidence to justify their position on each of these three subjects. Nevertheless, the evidence brought to bear is often speculative, anachronistic, or unconvincing due to the weight of counterevidence.

Jesus son of Joseph: From Galilee or From Judea?

The key to the controversial findings of *The Lost Tomb of Jesus* and *The Jesus Family Tomb* is identification of *Yeshua bar Yehosef* with the biblical figure of Jesus of Nazareth. As discussed previously, there is certainly no academic consensus with regard to the reading of the inscription on the ostensible Jesus ossuary. Nevertheless, even if the inscription *Yeshua bar Yehosef*, or "Jesus, son of Joseph," is admitted as properly read and translated, the evidence suggesting that this cannot be Jesus Christ is still considerable.

Consider the portion of the inscription, *bar Yehosef*. Even if the identity of the referent of "son of Joseph" is shown to be *Yeshua*, or 'Jesus,' the very use of "son of" in this context poses a virtually insurmountable difficulty with regard to common first century Israeli burial practices.

Cultural practices often vary on a regional basis, even within the boundaries of a single nation. One might witness, for example, the vastly different lifestyles of urban versus rural residents, even in the United States. Furthermore, those living in California may have drastically different views and customs than those living in Virginia, even though both are coastal states. Similar differences in customs with regard to burial practices might be expected, or at least allowed in theory, among people from the various regions in first century Israel.

Jodi Magness, a distinguished professor in the Department of Religious Studies at the University of North Carolina at Chapel Hill, has made a statement about first century Jewish burial practices that confirms the preceding discussion of varying cultural practices. Magness suggests that the inscription *Yeshua bar Yehosef* has the characteristics of an inscription for someone from Jerusalem or another part of Judea rather than having the characteristics of an inscription for a non-Judean, who would have been identified by place of origin rather than paternal lineage.

> "L. Y. Rahmani, an Israeli archaeologist who compiled a catalogue of all of the ossuaries in the collections of the state of Israel, observed that 'In Jerusalem's tombs, the deceased's place of origin was noted when someone from outside Jerusalem was interred in a local tomb.' On ossuaries in rock-cut tombs that belonged to Judean families, it was customary to indicate the ancestry or lineage of the deceased by naming the father, as, for example, Judah son of John (Yohanan); Honya son of Alexa; and Martha daughter of Hananya. But in rock-cut tombs owned by non-Judean families (or which contained the remains of relatives from outside Judea), it was customary to indicate the deceased's place of origin, as, for example, Simon of Ptolemais; Papias the Bethshanite (of Beth Shean); and Gaios son of Artemon from Berenike. Our historical and literary sources (such as the Gospels, Flavius Josephus, among others) often make the same distinctions between Judeans and non-Judeans (for example, Galileans, Idumaeans, Saul of Tarsus, Simon of Cyrene, and so on). If the Talpiyot tomb is indeed the tomb of Jesus and his family, we would expect at least some of the ossuary inscriptions to reflect their Galilean origins, by reading, for example, Jesus [son of Joseph] of Nazareth (or Jesus the Nazarene), Mary of Magdala,

> and so on. However, the inscriptions provide no indication that this is the tomb of a Galilean family and instead point to a Judean family." [120]

Joseph E. Zias, Senior Curator of Archaeology and Anthropology for the Israel Antiquities Authority (IAA) from 1972 to 1997, personally oversaw the cataloging the ossuaries from the Talpiot tomb. His conclusion is similar to that of Magness with regard to the scribe's use of *bar*, or "son of," rather than a place of origin.

> "The important thing to remember here is that individuals [from] outside of Judea, buried in Judea were named according to their place of origin, whereas in Judea this was not necessary. Had the names been Jesus of Nazareth, Mary of Nazareth, [Joseph of Nazareth, etc.,] I would have been totally convinced that this may be the family tomb, but as none of the names have place of origin, they are all Judeans." [121]

Thus, the common practice for burial in Judean tombs, such as that found in Talpiot, contradicts the possibility that the ossuary supposedly inscribed *Yeshua bar Yehosef* could be that of Jesus Christ. Jesus, raised in Nazareth in the region of Galilee, was not considered a Judean. According to the gospel of Matthew, Jesus' geographical origins were no mystery to the people.

> "Now Peter sat outside in the courtyard. And a servant girl came to him, saying, 'You also were with Jesus of Galilee.'" [122]

If a servant girl knew that Jesus' home was in Galilee, then, *a fortiori*, his family and close followers would also have known. Unless a convincing reason can be proffered for departure from common burial practices in this case, then it would be expected that an ossuary for Jesus Christ would be marked "Jesus of Galilee" or "Jesus of Nazareth" rather than "Jesus, son of Joseph."

Furthermore, since the region of Galilee, in the first century, was separated from Judea by Samaria, there can be no mistaking Nazareth for a Judean town. Thus, identification of the Talpiot ossuaries with Jesus' family contradicts common burial practices in first century Judea.

---

[120] Jodi Magness, "Has the Tomb of Jesus Been Discovered?" http://www.sbl-site.org/Article.aspx?ArticleId=640

[121] Joe Zias, "[Viewer's] guide to the Talpiot Tomb documentary," http://www.joezias.com/tomb.html

[122] Matthew 26:69 (NKJV)

As a result, even though the name *Yeshua bar Yehosef*, "Jesus, son of Joseph," is similar to that of the biblical figure of Jesus Christ, the content of the inscription does not conform to Judean burial customs at the time of Jesus' death. Since *The Jesus Family Tomb* provides no cogent reason why the common customs would have been ignored in this case, the conclusion that the ossuary was that of Jesus Christ is a blatant case of special pleading.

Mary, Joseph, and Matthew: What Evidence?

With regard to *Yose*, 'Joseph,' and *Matya*, 'Matthew,' *The Jesus Family Tomb* presents only speculation. Since speculation only presents possibilities rather than evidence, countering the claims of the authors is quite simple.

If *Yose* was Joseph, father of Jesus, then the possibility that he was buried in Nazareth is easily conceivable, given his residence there at the time of Jesus' birth. If *Yose* was the brother of Jesus, then there is little information from the Bible regarding his life and death. His burial might have been virtually anywhere in Israel or beyond. In either case, *The Jesus Family Tomb* presents no evidence that *Yose* died or was buried in Jerusalem, short of the circular reasoning that states that the ossuary inscribed with *Yose* must be that of Jesus' brother or father, because the other ossuary belongs to Jesus. Since no evidence is proffered, the claim that the death of *Yose* was in Nazareth is equally plausible, and no legitimate conclusion can be reached.

With regard to Matthew, the claim that the inscription *Matya* fits with the Jesus family, simply because Mary had a number of 'Matthews' in her genealogy, is specious, at best. One might equally claim that Mary wanted to avoid further use of Matthew for precisely the same reason. Such speculation may be undertaken ad nauseum; evidence, however, is required to substantiate the claims. There is no record of Mary having a son named Matthew, nor is there any evidence that there was a Matthew anywhere else in Jesus' immediate family. Such speculation need only be answered with a child-like response: "Prove it."

Further, according to the documentary, later Christian tradition suggests that Jesus' mother, Mary, was buried in Jerusalem. Neither the source of this tradition nor the time frame of 'later' is specified, however. Countering this claim is Paul L. Maier, Professor of Ancient History at Western Michigan University. Maier questions the burial of Mary in the same place where her son, Jesus, was murdered, and considers the matter in light of Church tradition and the early Christian historian Eusebius of Caesarea.

> "Why in the world would the 'Jesus Family' have a burial site in Jerusalem, of all places, the very city that crucified Jesus? Galilee was their home. In Galilee they might have had such a family burial site, not Judea. . . . Equating 'Maria' as Mary the mother of Jesus? Church tradition and the earliest Christian historian, Eusebius of Caesarea, are unanimous in reporting that Mary, the mother of Jesus, died in Ephesus, where the apostle John, faithful to his commission from Jesus on the cross, had accompanied her." [123]

Additionally, the question of the status of Jesus' family must be raised. Jesus and his family were nowhere identified as rich and, therefore, capable of purchasing luxuries such as a large, ornate family tomb. Maier further attests to this fact.

> "The 'Jesus Family' simply could not have afforded the large crypt uncovered at Talpiot, which housed, or could have housed, 200 ossuaries. This is the burial site of a prominent, wealthy family from Jerusalem, not a carpenter's clan from Galilee." [124]

The before-mentioned Magness makes a similar finding with regard to the financial status of the owners of the Talpiot tomb.

> "The work was all done by hand (using iron tools), cut into hard rock (limestone and dolomite). The notion that most Jews in Jerusalem owned rock-cut tombs is erroneous, and Tabor's claim that the tomb was 'modest' is irrelevant. Only the upper classes – a small segment of the population – owned rock-cut tombs." [125]

Contrary to the speculation presented in the film, the circumstances surrounding Jesus' family make it highly implausible that an ornate family tomb in Jerusalem was used to inter the remains of a relatively poor carpenter's family from Galilee. Furthermore, the presence of the inscription *Matya* poses continued difficulty so long as no rational explanation is proffered to justify the presence of such a name in the ostensible tomb of Jesus Christ's family.

---

[123] Laurence Gardner, "The Jesus Ossuary" (March 2007)

[124] *Ibid.*

[125] E-mail correspondence

Chapter Six: 3rd claim – Jesus' Family Burial In Jerusalem

> "[Matya] is not a known member of Jesus' family." [126]

Immediate Family or Multigenerational Family?

One of the key, although unstated, assumptions of the hypothesis concerning the Talpiot tomb is that the ossuaries contained only members of an immediate family. This claim, however, is not justified without evidence.

Contradicting this crucial assumption is Dr. Christopher A. Rollston, Professor of Old Testament and Semitic Studies at the Emmanuel School of Religion in Johnson City, Tennessee. His claim is that the kind of "nuclear family" paradigm associated with modern western civilization cannot be imposed on first century Jewish civilization without sufficient evidence.

> "Note, however, that for these six inscribed ossuaries from the Talpiyot Tomb, there are just two personal names with patronymics: (1) Yehuda bar Yeshua' and (2) Yeshua' bar Yosep. This is a pivotal issue because without patronymics it is not possible for someone in the modern period to ascertain the precise kinship relationships of antiquity. To be sure, such tombs were 'family tombs,' but to assume that such a tomb represents some sort of nuclear family and to assume that one can discern the nature of the relationships within that family without empirical evidence is problematic. For example, the assumption of these scholars is that the Yoseh of the Yoseh Ossuary was the son of Yosep. However, there is no patronymic on this inscription and so to assume that Yoseh was the son of Yosep (and thus the brother of Jesus) is problematic. That is, Yoseh could be the son of Mattiyah, or the son of Yehudah, or the son of Yeshua'. Perhaps, he was the father of Maryah, or the father of Miriamne, or Mattiyah. Maybe he is the uncle of one of these. Perhaps, Yoseh was the son or father or brother or uncle of someone who was buried in one of the ossuaries that does not contain an inscription. It is possible to suggest that he was a cousin of someone in the tomb. Not all of these are mutually exclusive, but ultimately, because there is neither patronymic, statement of relationship (e.g., brother), or title, any suggestion about the relationship of Yoseh to those interred here remains conjecture and speculation." [127]

Furthermore, Rollston, who has performed research at museums throughout the world and has participated as a staff member in archaeological excavations in such places as Tel Megiddo in Israel, continues with regard to Mary.

> "Similarly, for Maryah, the assumption of those propounding that this is the family tomb of Jesus of Nazareth is that this woman is the mother of Yeshua'

---

[126] *The Lost Tomb of Jesus*, The Discovery Channel (2007)

[127] Christopher A. Rollston, "Prosopography and the Talpiyot Yeshua Family Tomb: Pensées of a Palaeographer," http://www.sbl-site.org/Article.aspx?ArticleId=649

> bar Yosep. However, it is tenable to suggest that she was the wife of Yehudah, or the wife of Yoseh, or the wife of Mattiyah, or the wife of Yeshua'. She might have been the benevolent and kind aunt of someone buried in the tomb. She might have been the cousin of someone buried in the tomb. Sometimes we have complementary data. For example, an ossuary from the Kidron Valley is inscribed with the words: 'Shalom, wife of Yehudah.' However, for Maryah we simply do not have such data; thus, to assume that a modern scholar can discern and make an affirmation about the nature of some relationship is risible." [128]

If the Talpiot tomb is indeed multigenerational, then the difficulty associated with identifying the names on the ossuaries with Jesus Christ and his family grows tremendously. For example, the *Yeshua* as son of *Yehosef* may be different than the *Yeshua* as father of *Yehuda*, since, as pointed out in the documentary, names may be common on a generational basis within families.

The number of different possible relationships among people in an extended family, especially when more than a few generations are considered, makes the specificity of the relationships claimed in the book and documentary seem ludicrous. The unwarranted restriction of the examination of the names inscribed on the ossuaries to nuclear family members highly skews the investigation, especially with regard to the statistical calculations made later.

Attempts to mitigate this difficulty by appealing to the limited time span during which ossuaries were used are not convincing, however. President of La Sierra University in California, Dr. Lawrence T. Geraty, whose distinguished career has included service as professor in archaeology and history of antiquity as well as advisor on archaeology to former Crown Prince Hassan of Jordan, raises a further problem.

> "Jews buried bodies in the soil or in coffins until the flesh had [desiccated] and disappeared. Those who were particularly religious often then harvested the bones and stuffed them into these bone boxes (first century BC through second century AD) and shipped them off to Jerusalem to be buried near the Mount of Olives where they would be in close proximity to the place where Messiah would come – and eventually give them eternal life at the resurrection." [129]

Thus, a family tomb might have been decades or even more than a century old. In such a case, the number of sets of

---

[128] *Ibid.*

[129] E-mail correspondence (March 2, 2007)

bones interred could be vast, and the number of generations present also large. The time frame cited by Geraty is nearly three hundred years for the use of bone boxes, leaving plenty of time for a family to inter a large number of bodies from many generations.

> "There is NO evidence whatsoever that these are the remains or the tomb of anyone connected with Jesus of the New Testament. Just because the DNA shows the main characters were not related by blood doesn't mean they were married! Tombs were used and then reused. I excavated a similar tomb where there were 40 bodies buried over the course of many years." [130]

The use of ossuaries into the second century A.D. is suggested in discussion of archaeological finds in Galilee at Tiberias and Tzippori.

> "One ossuary was found. Small finds dated the tomb to the late-first/early-second century." [131]

> "Stone ossuaries, found in one of the recently excavated tombs, demonstrate Jewish burial customs in the second century [A.D.], as do Jewish inscriptions in some tombs." [132]

The question of the immediacy of the relationships among those interred in the Talpiot tomb is thus raised with no apparent method of resolution. That is to say, any attempt to definitely establish the relationships of those whose names were inscribed on the ossuaries is, once again, pure speculation without evidentiary support.

The Body of Jesus Christ

The biblical account of events that transpired after Jesus' crucifixion raises questions as to whether his body could have been stolen. The authors of *The Jesus Family Tomb* suggest, more implicitly than explicitly, that theft took place, contrary to the gospel account of Matthew. Nevertheless, success in such an exploit by a rabble of followers poses several difficulties.

Jesus Christ was crucified as a revolutionary who was perceived to pose a threat to Rome and to Caesar. As such, his

---

[130] E-mail correspondence (March 02, 2007)

[131] http://pace.cns.yorku.ca/York/york/placePopup?id=253

[132] http://pace.cns.yorku.ca/York/york/placePopup?id=285&descOnly=true

body was securely entombed and guarded following his crucifixion, in the prior knowledge that theft of his body might take place in order to facilitate proclamation of his resurrection. According to Matthew, the Jews and Romans were both aware of Jesus' claim that he would be resurrected, so they took steps to prevent any trickery.

> "The chief priests and Pharisees gathered together to Pilate, saying, 'Sir, we remember, while He was still alive, how that deceiver said, "After three days I will rise." Therefore command that the tomb be made secure until the third day, lest His disciples come by night and steal Him away, and say to the people, "He has risen from the dead." So the last deception will be worse than the first.' Pilate said to them, 'You have a guard, go your way, make it as secure as you know how.' So they went and made the tomb secure, sealing the stone and setting the guard." [133]

The requirement here was not to guard Jesus' body forever, but for three days: a very simple task designed to prevent deception on the part of Jesus' followers and to secure the integrity of Rome and Caesar. Also, the Roman 'guard' cited here was not singular, but a number of soldiers. It stretches credulity, then, to suggest that Jesus' followers, who apparently did not have an expectation of his resurrection, made a surreptitious bid to steal Jesus' body, despite the presence of Roman guards and, likely, other watchers as well.

Further difficulties with the prospect of Jesus' followers stealing his body are presented by Dr. Darrell L. Bock, research professor of New Testament studies and professor of spiritual development and culture at Dallas Theological Seminary in Texas.

> "Third, we have to accept that as the mourning family scrambled to steal the body from Joseph of Arimathea's tomb (where several knew the body was originally placed) and yet they preached an empty tomb and resurrection when they actually knew that Jesus was not raised, doing so at the risk of their own lives as Jesus' half brother's death (James) in AD 62 shows. This scenario for the hypothesis' truth involves several assumptions, the absence of any of which destroys the claim. Let's repeat this: they had to SECRETLY buy the tomb space from someone, prepare an ossuary over a year's period and then choose to adorn this ossuary of Jesus with graffiti-like script to name their dead hero. Surely if they had a year to prepare honoring Jesus, whom they had highly regarded, they would have adorned his ossuary with more than a mere graffiti like description. Note how some of the other ossuaries in this tomb are quite adorned, as pictures from the press conference showed. Not to mention that some of the family died for this belief, when they really knew Jesus had not left the tomb empty. This scenario as a whole seems quite implausible. I have not even raised the issue of Jesus' family being able to afford such a tomb, since

---

[133] Matthew 27:62-66

> they were at best lower middle class and these are upper echelon tombs ([if a] wealthy [benefactor] gave them this site, then there are people in Jerusalem who know where this site is and the secrecy of the locale is lost)." [134]

Conclusion

The common burial practices of first century Judea, the lack of evidence supporting claims concerning the burial locale of Mary and Joseph, the lack of any support for suggesting that there was a Matthew in Jesus' immediate family, and the tremendous feat that would have been required to steal and bury the deceased Jesus of Nazareth in an orderly fashion leads to a single conclusion: the hypothesis of *The Jesus Family Tomb* falls apart unless greater evidence is marshaled. Nevertheless, it remains to also investigate the authors' claim with regard to another key figure: Mary Magdalene.

---

[134] Darrel L. Bock, *"Hollywood Hype: The Oscars and Jesus' Family Tomb, What Do They Share?"* http://dev.bible.org/bock/node/106 (February 2007)

David's Judgment Seat, Jerusalem
(Source: Félix Bonfils)

STUDY QUESTIONS:

1. Why was Jesus referred to as "Jesus of Nazareth" or Jesus from Galilee when he was traveling in Judea?

2. What was the financial status of those that owned rocked carved tombs, wealthy or poor?

3. Being born where animals slept and fed (manger), and being a carpenter's son, would you consider Jesus of Nazareth as wealthy?

fourth claim: Mariamene e Mara is Mary Magdalene?

"The inscription does not read 'Mariamene the Master' nor does the name Mariamene or Mariamne appear on the ossuary at all."
-Dr. Stephen J. Pfann,
President of the University of the Holy Land in Jerusalem

If, for the sake of the discussion, it is granted that *Mariamene e Mara* is the correct reading of the markings on the Greek-inscribed ossuary from the Talpiot tomb, the difficulty of connecting this name to Mary Magdalene still remains. Furthermore, even if Mary Magdalene did, indeed, go by the name *Mariamene e Mara*, it is question-begging to simply state that she was the one interred in the *Mariamene* ossuary. The hypothesis under consideration is that Jesus Christ was buried in the Talpiot tomb; association of Mary Magdalene with the tomb must be based on evidence that does not rely on the assumption that the tomb also contains the remnants of Jesus. As such, further consultation with the remarks of scholars is in order.

The use of Greek for the inscription of the ossuary theorized as that of Mary Magdalene was justified in the documentary by way of reference to her home city, Migdal (or Magdala), which is said to have been bilingual. Nevertheless, even if Mary Magdalene had been fluent in Greek, it is highly unlikely that those who buried her in Judea would have spoken Greek as well. This notion is corroborated by Dr. Ben Witherington, New Testament scholar and colleague of Simcha Jacobovici in the 2002 investigation of the James ossuary.

"The earliest Jewish Christians in Jerusalem, including the members of Jesus'

> family and Mary Magdalene, did not speak Greek. They spoke Aramaic. We have absolutely no historical evidence to suggest Mary Magdalene would have been called by a Greek name before A.D. 70. She grew up in a Jewish fishing village called Migdal, not a Greek city at all. It makes no sense that her ossuary would have a Greek inscription and that of her alleged husband an Aramaic inscription." [135]

Even if it is assumed that Mary Magdalene could speak Greek and that those who buried her might have inscribed her name in Greek, even greater difficulties persist.

Acts of Philip: Abuse of a Scholar's Words

The Gnostic apocryphal book, Acts of Philip, was relied upon heavily in *The Jesus Family Tomb* and *The Lost Tomb of Jesus* when making the connection between *Mariamene e Mara* and Mary Magdalene. Dr. François Bovon, who in 1974 found a fourteenth century manuscript of the Acts of Philip, was quoted in *The Jesus Family Tomb* in a manner that seemed to indicate his association of the name *Mariamene*, or Mariamne, with Mary Magdalene.

> "This Mary Magdalene, this Mary from the Acts of Philip, is clearly the equal of the other apostle — and, as depicted, is even more enlightened than Philip." [136]

Ronald V. Huggins, associate professor of theological and historical studies at Salt Lake Theological Seminary in Utah, has discussed the tactics used in *The Jesus Family Tomb* with regard to citation of Bovon's statements.

> "I emailed Professor King and Professor Bovon on the point. . . . Both responded by denying that they ever said that Mariamne was Mary Magdalene's real name. What Bovon actually contends is that the figure Mariamne mentioned in the fourth century Acts of Philip *represented* Mary Magdalene." [137]

---

[135] Ben Witherington, "Problems Multiply for the Jesus Tomb Theory," http://benwitherington.blogspot.com/2007/02/problems-multiple-for-jesus-tomb-theory.html (February 2007)

[136] Simcha Jacobovici and Charles Pellegrino, *The Jesus Family Tomb* (2007) p. 97

[137] Ronald V. Huggins, "The Devil's in the Details: A Review of *The Jesus Family Tomb* and *The Lost Tomb of Jesus*," http://www.irr.org/Huggins-Jesus-tomb.pdf (2007)

Thus, although Bovon may have suggested that the Mariamne of the Acts of Philip may have represented Mary Magdalene, he did not claim an unequivocal identification.

> "I do not believe that Mariamne is the real name of Mary of Magdalene. Mariamne is, besides Maria or Mariam, a possible Greek equivalent, attested by Josephus, Origen, and the Acts of Philip, for the Semitic Myriam."[138]

Furthermore, Bovon goes on to clearly state his interest, with regard to Mariamne and Mary Magdalene, as being literary rather than historical.

> "This portrayal of Mariamne fits very well with the portrayal of Mary of Magdala in the Manichean Psalms, the Gospel of Mary, and Pistis Sophia. My interest is not historical, but on the level of literary traditions. I have suggested this identification in 1984 already in an article of New Testament Studies."[139]

The use of this literary perspective as a foundational claim in a historical context is completely unwarranted. As a result, there is no scholarly support for the unequivocal identification of the name Mariamne with Mary Magdalene. Hence, Craig A. Evans, Payzant Distinguished Professor of New Testament at Acadia Divinity College of Acadia University in Canada, appropriately rejects the use of the Acts of Philip in support of this claim.

> "The argument that this person is Mary Magdalene, on the strength of the 4th century Acts of Philip, is completely unpersuasive."[140]

Evans also cites a statement from Bovon regarding a logical leap made in *The Lost Tomb of Jesus* that was based on his words about the final resting place of Mariamne.

> "Bovon further notes that the Mariamne of the Acts of Philip, after her missionary journeys ultimately returns home to the Jordan Valley, and that her coffin is actually placed in the Jordan river itself. Jacobovici again misrepresents what Bovon had told him about this by saying, 'Mary Magdalene returned to Jerusalem and ended her days there. Clearly, the Talpiot tomb is consistent with

---

[138] François Bovon, *"The Tomb of Jesus,"* http://www.sbl-site.org/Article.aspx?ArticleId=656 (2007)

[139] *Ibid.*

[140] Ronald V. Huggins, "The Devil's in the Details: A Review of *The Jesus Family Tomb* and *The Lost Tomb of Jesus*," http://www.irr.org/Huggins-Jesus-tomb.pdf (2007)

> this tradition.' Again, however, Bovon afterward contradicted him: 'I said that the Acts of Philip sends her to the Jordan Valley, but the filmmaker concludes that this means Jerusalem!'"[141]

A simple look at a map of Israel shows that, far from being the sole province of Jerusalem, the Jordan Valley covers a rather large swath of land. This misrepresentation of Bovon is, perhaps, more egregious than that with regard to the identification of Mariamne with Mary Magdalene.

From this information alone, it becomes plain that one of the key premises of the argument that the Talpiot tomb is that of Jesus relies on the misuse of a scholar's words. Perhaps worse than just the damage to the case is the questions that must then be raised with regard to the integrity of the authors. Bovon relates his own perception of the way he was used in the documentary.

> "When I was questioned by Simcha Jacobovici and his team the questions were directed toward the Acts of Philip and the role of Mariamne in this text. I was not informed of the whole program and the orientation of the script. [Also,] having watched the film, in listening to it, I hear two voices, a kind of *double discours*. On one hand there is the wish to open a scholarly discussion; on the other there is the wish to push a personal agenda."[142]

This willingness to twist words to fabricate or exaggerate evidence smacks of either personal bias or preconceived opinions with regard to the Talpiot tomb and the person of Jesus Christ. It is at this point that one must begin to question whether the worldviews of the authors have not influenced them to the point of taking dishonest tactics with regard to a central point of Christianity, a worldview that stands squarely against their own. The lack of evidence to support major claims, along with academically dishonest tactics, suggests that the hypothesis of *The Jesus Family Tomb* and *The Lost Tomb of Jesus* may be based less on scholarship, not on weight of evidence and research but more on wishful thinking and personal animosity.

Acts of Philip: A Reliable Source?

---

[141] *Ibid.*

[142] François Bovon, "*The Tomb of Jesus*," http://www.sbl-site.org/Article.aspx?ArticleId=656 (2007)

Other scholars have questioned the value of the book and the documentary, especially with regard to the subject of Mary Magdalene. Dr. Samuele Bacchiocchi, author of fifteen books and former professor of theology and church history in the Religion Department of Andrews University in Michigan, dismissed both the documentary and its reliance on the Acts of Philip.

> "No serious scholar is paying attention to this [documentary]. This is basically a documentary that builds upon [*The Da Vinci Code*] and continues to where the [*The Da Vinci Code*] is taking off. The Acts of Philip is from the fourth century."[143]

Evans makes a similar point while further emphasizing the unreliability of the Acts of Philip, both as an apocryphal book with unverified historical accuracy and as a late text too far removed from the 1st century events to be considered trustworthy.

> "Apocrypha books can provide useful information. The danger is to take them too seriously, as providing historically trustworthy information. Acts of Philip dates to the fourth century. All tradition in it is highly suspect. A 'Mariamne' in the Acts of Philip is said to be the sister of Philip. This is unfounded apocryphal tradition. . . . In any case, it is late fiction; no qualified scholarly thinks it takes us back to the early first century and helps us identify Mary Magdalene."[144]

Another scholar contends that the name Mariamne cannot be identified with Mary Magdalene, regardless of any intimation in the Acts of Philip. Dr. William H. Shea, medical doctor, biblical archaeologist at the Earth History Research Center in Texas, and former director of the Institute of Archaeology at Andrews University in Michigan, has raised this point.

> "One of the names that they have twisted into Mary Magdalene is Mariamne. This is completely false. That was a separate name and it was the name, for example of the last Jewish wife of Herod the Great, he had her killed about 27 BC. He also had her two sons, Alexander and Aristobulus executed about 7 BC. This brought the Jewish line of the Maccabees to an end since Herod was not of that line."[145]

---

[143] Personal phone conv. from Bacchiocchi

[144] E-mail correspondence (March 10, 2007)

[145] E-mail correspondence (March 2, 2007)

Even for non-scholars, a simple glance at the text of the Acts of Philip shows it to be a form of fantasy rather than a historical relation of the events in the life of a first century man.[146] Included in the story are the taming and conversion of a talking goat and leopard, along with the slaying of a dragon.

Conclusion

If the statements of the scholars cited here are to be given any weight, then it is clearly unwarranted to rely upon the Acts of Philip as the sole source connecting Mariamne, and thus *Mariamene*, with Mary Magdalene. Furthermore, the evidence that is presented in the book and documentary with regard to Mary Magdalene is shown to be rationalization of a presumed conclusion concerning the Talpiot tomb.

Rather than finding evidence that buttresses the conclusion that *Mariamene e Mara* refers to Mary Magdalene, thus providing support for the hypothesis that the tomb belonged to Jesus' family, the authors simply presumed that the hypothesis was true. They then proceeded to find some link between *Mariamene e Mara* and Mary Magdalene. As a result, a circular argument is created such that the tomb must belong to Jesus because Mary Magdalene's ossuary was found in it, and the ossuary must belong to Mary Magdalene because the tomb belongs to Jesus. It is no wonder, then, that the statistical analysis, to which the next discussion will now turn, is skewed so largely in favor of the conclusion: key evidence is presented that already assumes the veracity of the hypothesis!

It is worthy of note that the authors apply a double standard with regards to the authority of eyewitness accounts of the New Testament writers. They assume that the Scripture is true when it supports their agenda and false when it doesn't. This is obvious indication of predominating bias that bowdlerizes anything that goes against it. This even becomes more pronounced when one realizes that the authors would rather use as authority an apocryphal book that talks about a converted talking goat and a converted talking leopard, written 400 years after the fact (the crucifixion of Jesus) rather than use eyewitness testimony of the writers of the canonized New Testament whose historicity had

---

[146] "*Acts of Philip*," http://wesley.nnu.edu/biblical_studies/noncanon/acts/actphil.htm

been proven beyond a reasonable doubt.[147] This so called "documentary" hardly comes up to the level of responsible scholarship.

Archaeologist Dr. Jonathan Reed, Professor of Religion at the University of La Verne is justified when he said, "It's what I would call archeo-porn. It's very exciting, it's stimulating, you want to watch it, but deep down you know it's wrong."[148]

---

[147] Norman L. Geisler, Frank Turkey, *I Don't Have Enough Faith To Be An Atheist* (Illinois: Good News Publishers, 2004), pp 221-249.

[148] Jonathan L. Reed quoted from *Lost Tomb of Jesus: A Critical Look*, March 4, 2007.

STUDY QUESTIONS:

1. What does Dr. Bovon mean when he says his interest in *Acts of Philip* is literary not historical?

2. Why did Dr. Bovon release a public statement denouncing the hypothesis of the documentary?

3. With Dr. Bovon's public statement in mind, how credible are the filmmakers when they say Dr. Bovon's work literary interest makes their Mary Magdalene assumption valid?

4. Name the reasons why scholars reject the use of *Acts of Philip* as a historical source?

fifth claim – statistical analysis

> *"Taking into account the chances that these names would be clustered together in a family tomb, this statistical study concludes that the odds – on the most conservative basis – are 600 to 1 in favor of this being the JESUS FAMILY TOMB."*
> –"Statistics Overview" from website of *The Lost Tomb of Jesus*

Statistical analysis can serve both honest and dishonest ends. Since it relies on a mixture of mathematical calculations and linguistic statements, very careful attention must be paid to even the smallest details, lest the results be skewed by errors, inaccuracies, or falsehoods. The reliability of the assumptions made prior to the analysis, along with the way they are stated in words, is crucial to the acceptability of the results of the analysis.

Dr. Andrey Feuerverger, statistician from the University of Toronto, endorses this idea in regard to the evidence presented in *The Jesus Family Tomb*.

> "It is not in the purview of statistics to conclude whether or not this [tomb site] is that of the New Testament family. Any such conclusion much more rightfully belongs to the purview of biblical historical scholars who are in a much better position to assess the assumptions entering into such computations. A role of statistics here is just to attempt to assess the odds of an equally (or more) 'surprising' cluster of names arising purely by chance under certain random sampling assumptions, under certain historical assumptions, and under some reasonable definition for 'surprisingness.'"[149]

---

[149] Andrey Feuerverger, Open letter, http://fisher.utstat.toronto.edu/andrey/OfficeHrs.txt (March 12, 2007)

Chapter Eight: 5th claim - Statistical Analysis

When performing an analysis of a historical event, such as the burial of a number of persons in the Talpiot tomb some two thousand years ago, the only probabilities that may be discussed are conditional probabilities. That is, to present a probability analysis with regard to a past event, the analysis must be based on at least one conditional ('if') statement. This somewhat technical distinction results from the fact that, strictly speaking, a past event has a probability of either one or zero, it follows the Law of Excluded Middle: it either did or did not occur. Jesus Christ, for example, either was or was not buried in the tomb in East Talpiot; there is no other probability. Nevertheless, a probabilistic statement can be made based on assumptions. For example, a legitimate statement would be the following: "If Jesus Christ did not ascend bodily to heaven, and if he was buried somewhere in Jerusalem, then the probability that the Talpiot tomb is that of Jesus is X." Here, X is some number between zero and one, inclusive.

Thus, the probabilistic statement made at the end of the analysis in *The Jesus Family Tomb* and *The Lost Tomb of Jesus* must be examined in terms of its key assumptions, as they may or may not lend support to the numbers presented. Although the assumptions used in the analysis are occasionally stated, they are not always explicit. Perhaps the most fundamental assumption of the analysis is that Jesus Christ did not ascend bodily into heaven; had this event taken place, the probability of the tomb being Christ's would drop to zero or very nearly to zero immediately. Statistician Aleks Jakulin of Columbia University in New York City corroborates the dependency on assumptions with regard to this very matter.

> "A Christian would use [a probability for Jesus being in a tomb] equal [to] zero, because of ascension, so the discussion stops right there."[150]

In spite of the critical dependence of the analysis upon the belief that Jesus did not ascend bodily, no justification for this assumption is given. Regardless of any lack of sufficient reasoning in this matter, the statistical analysis can be shown to fall apart based on the faulty or misleading evidence presented in other areas.

---

[150] Christopher Mims, "Should You Accept the 600-to-One Odds That the Talpiot Tomb Belonged to Jesus?" http://www.sciam.com/article.cfm?articleID=14A3C2E6-E7F2-99DF-37A9AEC98FB0702A&pageNumber=1&catID=4 (March 2, 2007)

Assumptions

It is extremely difficult to assess each of the numerous misleading assumptions made by the authors, as they selectively cite New Testament texts (a subject that shall be treated in a later chapter). *The Jesus Family Tomb* ignores certain passages, but not others, and makes some arguments from silence, but not others still. This rubber-stamping of historical texts suggests that the results of the analysis are unreliable due to patent bias. Nevertheless, regardless of the biases involved, it is helpful to examine some of the more obvious assumptions.

The method used to calculate the conditional probability that the Talpiot tomb belongs to Jesus of Nazareth and his family is dependent almost exclusively on the six names inscribed on the ossuaries found within. The relationships of those interred are crucial considerations.

First, it is assumed that *Yeshua bar Yehosef* and *Yose* are brothers, with *Yose* being a contraction of *Yehosef* ('Joseph').[151] The Gospel of Mark is cited from the New Testament as evidence.

> "Is this not the carpenter, the Son of Mary, and brother of James, Joses, Judas, and Simon?"[152]

In *The Jesus Family Tomb*, while attempting to take a 'conservative' approach, *Yose* is treated as a contraction of *Yehosef*.

> "So I decided to agree with Kloner and to treat the 'Jos'e' inscription as just another 'Joseph' in the tomb."[153]

The attempt to maintain a conservative approach was taken in order to avoid numbers that, according to the Charles Pellegrino, "on a gut level... seemed too much." Given that the authors obviously came to the evidence with a preconceived conclusion, one might wonder why there is any necessity for a 'conservative' approach, which lowers the enormous numbers that are in their

---

[151] Amos Kloner, "A Tomb with Inscribed Ossuaries in East Talpiyot, Jerusalem," *Atiquot*, Vol. 29 (1996)

[152] Mark 6:3 (NKJV)

[153] Simcha Jacobovici and Charles Pellegrino, *The Jesus Family Tomb* (2007) p. 77-78

favor. This is almost certainly an attempt to mask the unwarranted assumptions, which were made without objective examination of the evidence, in order to prevent personal biases from becoming apparent. Regardless of the motivation, however, the assumption that *Yose* is a brother of Jesus is highly questionable.

Yose is not inscribed as *Yose bar Yehosef*, a symmetry that might be expected in a family tomb, thus casting doubt on the assumption that *Yose* was a brother of *Yeshua*. Furthermore, it is not even proposed as a possibility in the above-mentioned passage that *Yose* might be the same as *Yehosef*, father of *Yeshua*. It is certainly conceivable that a grieving wife may have had her husband's ossuary inscribed with a 'nickname,' even though her son's name might later have been inscribed along with his father's formal name. Furthermore, it is not suggested that *Yose* might be a cousin to *Yeshua*.

Perhaps the most curious fact is that, in spite of the rush to test DNA samples out of the *Yeshua* and *Mariamene* ossuaries, there was no test mentioned with regard to *Yeshua* and *Yose*. Brotherhood is simply assumed solely on the testimony of the Gospel of Mark, even though other portions of the book are ignored or contradicted. Since *Yose* is treated as brother to *Yeshua*, the use of a conditional probability factor for *Yose* is added to the calculation, thus aiding the conclusion of the book and documentary. Were *Yose* a cousin or father to *Yeshua*, then the presence of the *Yose* ossuary would be of no value.

Second, the assumption is made that *Mariamene e Mara* is Mary Magdalene. In this case, as discussed in the preceding chapter, the evidence cited in support of this assumption is two-fold unimpressive: the Acts of Philip, a fourteenth century text believed to have originated three centuries after the time of Jesus Christ, and the presumption that the tomb belonged to Jesus of Nazareth. With regard to the Acts of Philip, reliance on this text, with its dubious historical accuracy, has already been treated. The authors of *The Jesus Family Tomb* were found to have been deceptive and irrational in their sole reliance on the supposed relationship of Mariamne to Mary Magdalene. Their dependence upon this kind of flimsy evidence reveals the presumption that the Talpiot tomb is that of Jesus, since Mary Magdalene was assumed, beforehand, to have been *Mariamene*. The Acts of Philip has simply served as a rationalization of this presumption.

Since the relationship of *Mariamene e Mara* to *Yeshua* is thus indeterminate, the *Mariamene* ossuary cannot be of any benefit to the statistical analysis presented in *The Jesus Family Tomb*. Further, as Feuerverger stated in an interview with *Scientific American*, only if the assumptions are true can the statistics be considered appropriate.

> "With every assumption that was made an attempt was made to be reasonable. The two that I can't really say anything about because of the biblical scholarship part of it are the Mariemene e Mara -- how truly appropriate that is to Mary Magdalene, and how appropriate Yose is for one of the brothers of Jesus."[154]

Third, *Yehuda bar Yeshua* is considered to be the son of *Yeshua* and *Mariamene*, an additional unjustified conclusion. Rather than relying on the lack of a mention of a son of Jesus anywhere in the Gospels or other contemporaneous literature as potential evidence against the hypothesis, a conspiratorial rationalization was made.

> "'After they killed the fathers, they went after the kids,' [Jacobovici] said. 'The Romans didn't mess about. They called Jesus 'King of the Jews.' They mocked his royal lineage. Any surviving son would have been a target. He had to be hidden. That's why we haven't heard of him.'"[155]

Thus, by an argument from silence, a lack of evidence becomes evidence.

> "'It sounds like madness when you first hear it,' [James Cameron] thought aloud, 'but there's a certain logic to it. The existence of [Judah, or *Yehuda*] would have been concealed – probably even from most of the disciples – when Jesus was still alive. Concealed, probably, by Jesus's [*sic*] directive.'"[156]

Circular reasoning is always logical; it is not, however, informative. The assumption that Judah is the son of Jesus will always lead to the conclusion that Judah is the son of Jesus, especially if those making the argument wish to hold tenaciously to that assumption. Rather than being a disqualifying fact that virtually eliminates any possibility that the Talpiot tomb is that of Jesus

---

[154] Christopher Mims, "Should You Accept the 600-to-One Odds That the Talpiot Tomb Belonged to Jesus?" http://www.sciam.com/article.cfm?articleID=14A3C2E6-E7F2-99DF-37A9AEC98FB0702A&pageNumber=1&catID=4 (March 2, 2007)

[155] Simcha Jacobovici and Charles Pellegrino, *The Jesus Family Tomb* (2007) p. 90

[156] *Ibid.*

Christ, the presence of the name *Yehuda bar Yeshua* inscribed on the ossuary is simply discounted completely and does not enter into the calculations.

Dr. Randy Ingermanson, physicist and author, notes that the identification of *Yehuda* as the son of Jesus of Nazareth is a case of question-begging.

> "The authors of *The Jesus Family Tomb* argue at some length that this tomb shows that Jesus must have had a son. But the argument doesn't work that way. You have to first demonstrate that the Jesus in the tomb IS Jesus of Nazareth based on the evidence you have. And the evidence we have is that Jesus of Nazareth very likely didn't have a son."[157]

Jack Poirier, doctoral candidate at the Jewish Theological Seminary in New York City, makes a similar statement regarding the fallacious reasoning about *Mariamene e Mara* and *Yehuda bar Yeshua*.

> "In the end, in order to make their statistics work, we even have to accept that Jesus was married to Mary Magdalene and that the couple secretly had a child named 'Judah.' Rather than being treated as liabilities to a statistical study, these details are turned into historical givens and are even factored in as a positive match. Consequently, most of the connections made in the documentary fall under the heading of 'special pleading.'"[158]

Fourth, the presence of the *Matya* ossuary is ignored in the calculation since, according to Pellegrino, it is a name associated with the Jesus family.

> "'Matthew' was a common name in her family. It is, as James Tabor has argued, a priestly name, and Mary, by her relationship with Elizabeth, mother of John the Baptist, had a priestly connection. Also, Mary's grandfather was called Matthew, so it is entirely possible that, for example, a first cousin called Matthew, after the grandfather, might be buried in the family tomb. . . . Statistically, [the presence of the 'Matthew' inscription] didn't *invalidate* anything, but neither did it *validate* anything. I discounted it."[159]

---

[157] Randy Ingermanson, "Statistics and 'The Jesus Family Tomb,'" http://www.ingermanson.com/jesus/art/stats.php (2007)

[158] *Ibid.*

[159] Simcha Jacobovici and Charles Pellegrino, *The Jesus Family Tomb* (2007) p. 78

This kind of "my brother's mother's friend's son's etc." speculation is laughable. It is not remotely scientific, nor is it to be counted as relevant evidence. The presence of *Matya*, instead, may be counterevidence. If *Yose* is considered, without justification, to be the brother of *Yeshua*, then it is equally likely (unless preconceived opinions are brought to bear) that *Matya* is brother to *Yeshua*. Such a consideration could be made in light of the fact that *Yose*, ostensible brother to *Yeshua*, is not given a patronymic identification. The same is the case for *Matya*. If *Matya* is brother to *Yeshua*, however, the thesis that the tomb belongs to Jesus of Nazareth suffers extensive damage, since there is no record of *Matya* being son of Mary and Joseph. Rather than considering this possibility (or, for example, performing a DNA test on whatever remains could be found), the ossuary inscribed with *Matya* is simply ignored in the analysis.

The difficulty with the presence of the *Matya* ossuary is stated with a slightly different twist by Dr. Darrell L. Bock.

> "There is one name that has no evidence of being family, that is, Matthew. The claim is it "family related" only serves to show how the evidence is being handled in a very open ended way. Once we allow for the possibility of names outside the family to impact the site, we also have opened the door for non-family realities to impact the analysis. We, however, also undercut the claim this is really a family tomb. One cannot have it both ways. Once we [cease] to have a family tomb, then how do we analyze the names? If this is a family tomb, then what is Matthew doing in it. Either way, there is a problem with the identification."[160]

Thus, if the scope of 'family' allowed in the tomb is increased, the presence of the already common names becomes increasingly unremarkable. *The Jesus Family Tomb*, however, attempts both to expand the types of relationships allowed among those interred in the tomb and, simultaneously, to limit them with regard to some of the names. Such an approach is simply a case of special pleading.

These four assumptions, shown here to be unwarranted, speculative, or question-begging, are crucial factors in the conditional probability calculations used in *The Jesus Family Tomb* and *The Lost Tomb of Jesus*. Only when these assumptions are made can the statistical calculations be as simple as multiplication of the

---

[160] Darrell L. Bock, "Response to Tabor's Remarks on Statistics," http://dev.bible.org/bock/node/143 (March 26, 2007)

estimated relative frequencies of names in first century Israel. The final result of six hundred to one odds in favor of the tomb being that of Jesus Christ is actually a conditional probability. The probability is six hundred to one, conditional (that is, dependent) on the acceptability of the assumptions. If the assumptions are shown to be unwarranted, as they have been here, the conditional probability is a number that has absolutely nothing to do with the reality of the Talpiot tomb.

Since, as previously discussed, the names inscribed on the ossuaries in the tomb correspond to people who may have been in any number of different relationships, calculation of an accurate conditional probability must incorporate this fact. Furthermore, the number of possible relationships increases due to a multigenerational time span.

Frequency of Names and the "Jesus Equation"

The numbers most prominently discussed in the documentary are the frequencies of names as estimated for first century Israel. As pointed out by Ingermanson, there are no recorded lists of names for ancient Israel. As a result, other sources must be consulted for an estimate of the relative frequencies of various names in the Jewish onomasticon.

> "We don't have census data for ancient Jerusalem. What we do have are some surveys taken from various sources that list how often certain names appear. Two lists have been compiled by Israeli scholars, one by Dr. Rachel Hachlili and one by Dr. Tal Ilan."[161]

While the lists mentioned by Ingermanson differ slightly, even if the more conservative numbers are accepted (that is, those numbers most favorable to the thesis of *The Jesus Family Tomb*), the arbitrary nature of the assumptions that go into the equation still remain an overwhelming negative factor.

The conditional probability calculation used to produce the odds of six hundred to one in favor of the thesis of the book includes Jesus, son of Joseph, Mariamne, Yose, and Maria. As mentioned, identification of Mariamne with Mary Magdalene is

---

[161] Randy Ingermanson, "Bayes' Theorem And The 'Jesus Family Tomb,'" http://www.ingermanson.com/jesus/art/stats2.php (2007)

tenuous, at best. Also, exact identification of Yose in relation to Jesus, son of Joseph is also speculative. Eliminating both of these as unsubstantiated claims and simply omitting them from the calculation leads to a vastly different number when the bias factor of four and the adjustment factor of one thousand, accounting for the total number of tombs, are considered. The new conditional probability is about five to one against the tomb being that of Jesus Christ. Far from being convincing with regard to the hypothesis of the book, this number is moderately compelling to the contrary.

Nevertheless, the number above must be considered to be the very best odds, as the conditional probability that names like *Matya* and *Yehuda bar Yeshua* could be evidence against the hypothesis must also be considered. In light of the highly speculative nature of the arguments presented in favor of simply ignoring these names, rather than using them in the calculations as evidence against the hypothesis, the conditional probability is, in all likelihood, much greater than five to one against the conclusion that the Talpiot tomb is the Jesus family tomb.

Conclusion

Feuerverger, in an interview with *Scientific American*, reiterated his position that the calculations presented in *The Jesus Family Tomb* and *The Lost Tomb of Jesus*, for which Feuerverger was given credit, are dependent upon the assumptions brought to the analysis.

> "I have to tell you that a statistician working with a subject matter expert, in this case biblical historical scholars, essentially is obliged to rely on assumptions that come from them. It's not a secret that the assumptions are contestable. I tried to stay with things that vaguely seemed reasonable to me, but I'm not a biblical scholar. At the end of the day, I went with specific assumptions and I try to make clear what those assumptions were."[162]

Therefore, the burden of explanation rests not so much with Feuerverger, although he may have been more or less complicit in failing to question misleading assumptions, but with the authors who were the sources of the assumptions. As discussed

---

[162] Christopher Mims, "Should You Accept the 600-to-One Odds That the Talpiot Tomb Belonged to Jesus?" http://www.sciam.com/article.cfm?articleID=14A3C2E6-E7F2-99DF-37A9AEC98FB0702A&pageNumber=1&catID=4 (March 2, 2007)

above in some detail, the assumptions that underlie the ostensible six hundred to one odds are based on extremely dubious evidence and, additionally, often fail to consider other likely possibilities. Thus, Feuerverger's dissociation from the conclusions of the book and film is appropriate.

> "In this respect I now believe that I should not assert any conclusions connecting this tomb with any hypothetical one of the NT family. The interpretation of the computation should be that it is estimating the probability of there having been another family at the time, living in Jerusalem, whose tomb would be at least as 'surprising', under certain specified assumptions."[163]

---

[163] Andrey Feuerverger, Open letter, http://fisher.utstat.toronto.edu/andrey/OfficeHrs.txt (March 12, 2007)

STATISTICS TABLE									
FREQUENCY OF NAMES									
Jesus Son of Joseph	Mariamne		Matia		Yose		Maria		
1 in 190	1 in 160		1 in 40		1 in 20		1 in 4		
INITIAL COMPUTATION									
Jesus Son of Joseph	Mariamne		Matia		Yose		Maria		
1/190 x	1/160	x	1/40	x	1/20	x	1/4	=	1/97,280,000
SECOND COMPUTATION (Eliminating Matia since he is not explicatively mentioned in the Gospels)									
Jesus Son of Joseph	Mariamne		Yose		Maria				
1/190 x	1/160	x	1/20	x	1/4			=	1/2,400,000
THIRD COMPUTATION (Adjusting for unintentional biases in the historical sources)									
2,400,000 ÷ 4								=	600,000
FOURTH COMPUTATION (Adjust for all possible First Century Jerusalem Tombs)									
600,000 ÷ 1,000								=	600
PROBABILITY FACTOR = 600 to 1									

Statistics Formula
(Source: Discovery Channel)

Chapter Eight: 5th claim - Statistical Analysis

STUDY QUESTIONS:

1. What happens if one assumption is proven to be incorrect, what would happen to the results?

2. Why are two of the six ossuary names conveniently ignored in the equation?

3. If the tomb was multi-generational and these individuals are not immediately related as the documentary claims, what happens to the 'probability'?

sixth claim: DNA evidence

"'DNA analysis conducted at one of the world's foremost molecular genetics laboratories...suggests a 2,000-year-old Jerusalem tomb could have once held the remains of Jesus of Nazareth and his family."
-Press Release

The use of DNA analysis in recent years has become both a highly used source of evidence in civil and criminal cases as well as a popular symbol in entertainment for advanced identification methods. The use of DNA analysis in *The Jesus Family Tomb* and *The Lost Tomb of Jesus* provide a popular appeal, in addition to a scientific aura. Nevertheless, in spite of appearances, the results of the DNA test only provide as much information as the assumptions brought to the case allow. Proper interpretation of the results is critical.

      The process of drawing legitimate conclusions from DNA analysis involves accurately answering three questions. First, what exactly is being tested? Second, what are the results of the DNA test? Third, how are the results to be interpreted? Imprecise or unjustified answers to any of these questions can lead to conclusions that are false or misleading. Readers may judge for themselves whether Dr. Charles Pellegrino was being honest or disingenuous when he described the approach to DNA analysis.

> "To begin, the DNA tests were designed based on doubt, and were intended to disprove this tomb, not to prove anything. They are merely one brief chapter in a series of attempted disproofs."[164]

---

[164] Charles Pellegrino, Review of *The JEsus Family Tomb* at Amazon.com, http://www.amazon.com/gp/cdp/member-reviews/ATCK44DII6CW/ref=cm_cr_auth/103-1620597-6775031?ie=UTF8&sort%5Fby=MostRecentReview (March 6, 2007)

What Was Tested?

The first question that must be addressed with regard to the DNA analysis is with regard to the source of the DNA. Although DNA was extracted from the ossuaries, there is no guarantee that the source of the DNA was the person whose name was inscribed on the ossuary. Perhaps the most glaring difficulty is that ossuaries are not environmentally isolated vessels. Various contaminants, both of a biological and non-biological nature, as well as other factors such as humidity and temperature, can have a substantial effect on materials. This is especially true for human remains that are thousands of years old.

Given that, as previously mentioned, the authors of *The Jesus Family Tomb* admit to the presence of looters or vandals in the tomb in antiquity, the contents of the ossuaries immediately become suspect.

> "Displacement of the seals and removal of the stones were sure signs that looters or vandals had entered the tomb at some point [in antiquity]."[165]

Yet, the fact that there had been looters or vandals that may have disturbed or contaminated the tomb does not seem to have any sway over the presentation of the DNA analysis. Dr. Randy Younker, professor and researcher at the Institute of Archaeology at Andrews University in Michigan reiterated this difficulty.

> "The tomb contained many parts of bones and bone boxes. When you're collecting residue for DNA testing, it could come from anybody buried there, or anyone who had tampered with the tomb from ancient times until today."[166]

In forensic science, "chain of custody" is the phrase used to describe the handling of evidence. To maintain the integrity of the sample, as well as the judicial process, very careful records are maintained concerning who handled, analyzed, or held custody of

---

[165] Simcha Jacobovici and Charles Pellegrino, *The Jesus Family Tomb* (2007) p. 9

[166] Elizabeth Lechleitner, "ANN Feature: 'Lost Tomb of Jesus' Discovered? 'Dig a Little Deeper,' Says Adventist Archaeologist," http://news.adventist.org/data/2007/02/1174483238/index.html.en (March 21, 2007)

the relevant materials. In the case of the Talpiot ossuaries, the chain of custody is suspect on several levels. First, vandalism could have taken place resulting in handling or misplacing of bones. Second, contamination during removal or inspection of the ossuaries in 1980 may also have occurred. This latter concern is doubly troublesome due to the claim that one of the ossuaries was stolen, later to be identified in the book and documentary as, quite possibly, the controversial James ossuary. This suggests, if true, a lapse of security at some point, if not at many points, regarding the storage of the ossuaries since 1980.

Beyond simply chain of custody issues, the question of contamination is critical. Contamination may not simply have been by vandals, those who excavated the tomb, and those who performed the DNA analysis. The intended presence of other bones is also a concern. In her report on the James ossuary, Dr. Rochelle I. Altman commented, offhand, that ossuaries sometimes held the bones of more than one individual.

> "There is a relationship between status and ossuary, but this does not reflect the wealth or social status of the encasketed individual(s) (up to three sets of same-family bones can be buried in one ossuary)."[167]

Also, Dr. Stephen J. Pfann noted than "an ossuary would often contain more than one individual's bones."[168] In his report in *Atiquot*, Amos Kloner also made a similar statement in passing.

> "The number of interments may be estimated at 35: 17 in the ossuaries (based on an average of 1.7 individuals per ossuary), and 18 outside the ossuaries. These figures are based on demographic data compiled by the author."[169]

In light of the possibility that the bones of a number of individuals could have been interred in any of the ossuaries, including that of *Yeshua bar Yehosef* and *Mariamene e Mara*, the identity of the source of the DNA becomes uncertain almost to the point that it is unknowable.

---

[167] Rochelle I. Altman, "Official Report on the James Ossuary," http://www.bibleinterp.com/articles/Official_Report.htm

[168] Stephen J. Pfann, "Mary Magdalene is Now Missing: A Corrected Reading of Rahmani Ossuary 701," http://www.uhl.ac/MariameAndMartha.pdf

[169] Amos Kloner, "A Tomb with Inscribed Ossuaries in East Talpiyot, Jerusalem," *Atiquot*, Vol. 29 (1996)

Additionally, there is also a question with regard to the integrity of DNA from biological matter that has been entombed for some two thousand years in a relatively warm climate. Dr. Ian Barnes of the School of Biological Sciences at Royal Holloway, University of London, suggests that the samples are almost assuredly unreliable.

> "DNA degrades over time. At high temperatures, it degrades even faster. I've worked in the Middle East [where] we did not have any success even a few hundred years back, let alone 2,000 years. What worries me most is that the sample they took was not from bones. . . . This is a 2,000-year-old tomb. The potential for contamination is clearly enormous. It is highly possible that the DNA belongs to someone who excavated the tomb."[170]

Barnes goes on to describe the difficulty of obtaining a reliable DNA sample from tombs in warm climates.

> "We think that we understand some of the basis for DNA decay. The [math] is quite laborious, but we recently published a paper stating that for DNA in bone, at an average temperature of 25 [degrees Celcius], we might expect to get a decent amount of DNA (enough to analyse properly) from material up to about 500 years old. If the tombs were cooler, then DNA will last longer. The figure of 25 [degrees Celcius] was for Egypt, as I've never been to Jerusalem I don't know if that might be too hot as an average. Egyptian tombs are typically hot and damp, again I don't know about these tombs. Basically, the DNA gets cooked. The hotter it is, the faster it gets cooked."[171]

While an analyzable DNA sample from a two thousand year old tomb is not entirely out of the question, certainly the matter merits greater consideration than was apparently given in the book and documentary.

Combined, all the difficulties discussed here suggest that it is highly unlikely that the DNA test analyzed was uncontaminated DNA from *Yeshua bar Yehosef* and *Mariamene e Mara*. Even if it is granted that these were the subjects of DNA testing, the conclusions that may be drawn from the results are still uncertain.

---

[170] James Morgan, "The DNA of Jesus? Don't be so sure, Mr Cameron," *The Herald*, http://www.theherald.co.uk/features/features/display.var.1226604.0.0.php (March 1, 2007)

[171] E-mail correspondence (2007)

What Were the Results?

Dr. Carney Matheson, forensic examiner and scientific officer at Lakehead University's Paleo-DNA Laboratory and associate professor in the Department of Anthropology, was in charge of the DNA analysis of the samples. He summarized his approach and the results of the test in a correspondence with Dr. James White of Alpha and Omega Ministries.

> "This work was done as a service. We did not know who they suspected these [samples] to be from. On the report it concludes that these two profiles from two different individuals were not maternally related. That is all the report states. When they did the filming and on the documentary they asked every question under the sun with permutations and manipulations. I provided the investigators with all the possibilities. They were not brother and sister, mother and child, maternal cousins, maternal grandparent and child etc. I also mentioned all of the possibilities, which I should not have done in hindsight. These included, father and daughter, paternal cousins, half brother and sister (sharing the same father) or simply unrelated individuals. The media does what they want."[172]

Thus, the test determined, based on mitochondrial DNA, that the individuals from whom the samples were obtained were not maternally related. There is no need to dispute the findings of the test, although the source of the samples and the integrity of the DNA from the tomb may be questionable matters. Of critical importance is the interpretation of these results.

How Are the Results To Be Interpreted?

In *The Jesus Family Tomb*, Matheson was simply quoted to the effect that, due to the family tomb context, the lack of maternal ancestry suggested a marital relationship.

> "This man and woman do not share the same mother. They cannot be mother and child. They cannot, maternally, be brother and sister. And so, for these particular samples, because they come from the same tomb – and we suspect it to be a familial tomb – these two individuals, if they were unrelated, would most likely have been husband and wife."[173]

---

[172] James White, "Dr. Carney Matheson Responds," http://www.aomin.org/index.php?itemid=1809 (March 2, 2007)

[173] Simcha Jacobovici and Charles Pellegrino, *The Jesus Family Tomb* (2007) p. 172

Chapter Nine: 6th claim - DNA Evidence

In a later statement, Matheson suggested that although he oversaw the DNA testing and presented the results, he did not believe there to be any overly informative findings.

> "The only conclusions we made was that these two sets were not maternally related. To me it sounds like absolutely nothing."[174]

Also, in a report by Ted Koppel examining the documentary *The Lost Tomb of Jesus*, Matheson is once again cited.

> "There is a statement in the film that has been taken out of context. While marriage is a possibility, other relationships, like father and daughter, paternal cousins, sister-in-law or indeed two unrelated individuals, are also possible."[175]

The significance of a negative finding with regard to the maternal ancestry of *Yeshua bar Yehosef* and *Mariamene e Mara* does very little to aid the case of the authors. While marriage is indeed a possible relationship, it is by no means the only possible relationship. It is curious that, as noted in the preceding chapter, although Charles Pellegrino specifically allows for the possibility of *Matya* being a cousin, apparently no consideration is given to the possibility that *Mariamene e Mara* is a cousin. Certainly this is possible, given the multi-generational use of family tombs, and the lack of any mention of this in the book or documentary smacks of preconceived opinion.

Additionally, the possibility of a half-sister and half-brother relationship is ignored. This is quite interesting in light of James D. Tabor's assertion in *The Jesus Dynasty* that Jesus was an illegitimate child by way of a Roman soldier.[176] Given Tabor's prominence and numerous citations in *The Jesus Family Tomb* and *The Lost Tomb of Jesus*, the utter silence about the various possibilities regarding the potential relationship of *Yeshua* and *Mariamene e Mara* is inexcusable.

---

[174] Christopher Mims, Scientificamerican.com blog, http://blog.sciam.com/index.php?title=says_scholar_whose_work_was_used_in_the&more=1&c=1&tb=1&pb=1 (March 2, 2007)

[175] Ted Koppel, "The Lost Tomb of Jesus: A Critical Look," The Discovery Channel (March 4, 2007)

[176] James D. Tabor, *The Jesus Dynasty*, Simon & Schuster (2006)

Conclusion

Given the shaky evidence, questionable assumptions, and unjustified conclusions with regard to the testing of DNA evidence, one might legitimately question whether "the DNA tests were designed based on doubt, and were intended to disprove this tomb, not to prove anything," as Pellegrino asserted. No attentive skeptic could possibly ignore the innumerable opportunities for legitimate doubt in this case.

Furthermore, the failure to conduct further tests indicates the disingenuous nature of the use of DNA testing as more of a crowd-pleasing prop than as legitimate science. The choice of test subjects and lack of control tests is also extremely suspicious. For example, why was there no test of *Yehuda bar Yeshua* and *Mariamene e Mara*? Would this not have been more convincing evidence, were *Yehuda* shown to be son of *Mariamene e Mara*? Why was *Yose*, supposedly brother to *Yeshua*, not tested? In both these cases, maternal relation could have been established. Nevertheless, no attempts were made.

To be fair to the authors, The *Jesus Family Tomb* does provide an explanation for this lack of further testing.

> "[Jacobovici] wanted few things more in the world now than to have a DNA sample from 'Judah, son of Jesus.' But sadly, despite repeated efforts, his path to a sample from [the Judah ossuary] appeared to be irreversibly blocked. No one was being particularly clear with him about what had happened to the bone material. By one account, the accretion bed had been scoured out of the Judah ossuary as part of a cleaning in preparation for a museum display of a random collection of ossuaries with typical New Testament names. By another account, DNA work might be possible in the future by swabbing stains on the ossuary walls."[177]

One wonders if the mysterious 'scouring' of an ancient, easily damaged archaeological relic is actually what took place, or whether a further attempt at building a conspiratorial atmosphere, perhaps at the expense of complete honesty, is being built. Nevertheless, no explanation of the lack of testing of other samples is given.

The motivations of the authors may be speculated upon, but can never be known, short of honest statements from the men themselves. The evidence, however, is available for public

---

[177] Simcha Jacobovici and Charles Pellegrino, *The Jesus Family Tomb* (2007) p. 174

inspection. It is quite clear that, in the case of DNA testing, precious little information has been gained toward the end of determining whether the Talpiot tomb once held the remains of Jesus of Nazareth.

The Jesus Tomb: Is It Fact or Fiction? Scholars Chime In

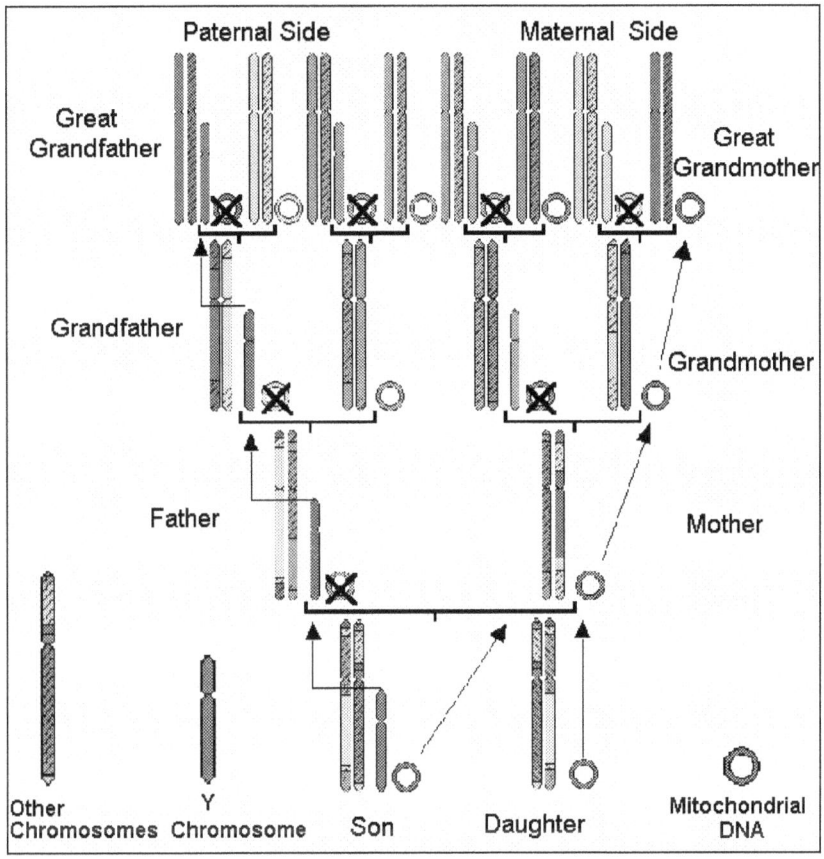

Mitochondrial DNA Tree
(Source: BassettDNA)

Chapter Nine: 6th claim - DNA Evidence

STUDY QUESTIONS:

1. Why is it problematic for DNA forensic experts that the tomb was looted or vandalized before the discovery in 1980?

2. Is there a possibility that the DNA samples may have been contaminated from other individuals working in the IAA warehouse or excavation site in 1980?

3. Why did the filmmakers conveniently neglect to mention the other relationship possibilities?

10

seventh claim: the James ossuary

"If the James ossuary can be traced back to the Talpiot tomb, the statistical case is closed."
-Simcha Jacobovici

In *The Lost Tomb of Jesus* and *The Jesus Family Tomb*, significant weight is placed upon connection of the James ossuary with the Talpiot tomb. First showcased on October 21, 2002, at a press conference sponsored by the Discovery Channel and the Biblical Archaeology Society, the James ossuary was presented as an historically remarkable discovery and the first archaeological evidence of the existence of Jesus. An official Israel Antiquities Authority (IAA) committee of scientists, however, determined that the inscription on the ossuary, *Ya'akov bar Yehosef akhui di Yeshua* ("James, son of Joseph, brother of Jesus"), was a modern forgery. Specifically, the inscription "brother of Jesus" was added. The announcement of the committee's findings was made at a press conference in Jerusalem on June 18, 2003. An Israeli antiquities collector, Oded Golan, was indicted for antiquities fraud on December 29, 2004.

    In spite of the fraud perpetrated with regard to this ossuary, and the concomitant fact that the ossuary had been in the hands con artists for an indefinite period of time, the James ossuary was still used in the book and documentary to build the case that the Talpiot tomb was that of Jesus Christ. Since there was indeed a James, brother of Jesus, noted in the New Testament texts, a connection between the ossuary, forgery notwithstanding, and the tomb would be added evidence in support of the hypothesis. To this end, attempts were made, through measurements and patina 'fingerprinting,' to link the James ossuary to the Talpiot tomb. The conclusion of *The Lost Tomb of Jesus* is that the James ossuary was, indeed, originally found in that controversial tomb.

> "The patina samples from the Talpiot tomb match with the James ossuary.... This is key evidence indicating the ossuary inscribed 'James, son of Joseph, brother of Jesus' is the missing ossuary from the Talpiot tomb."[178]

Nevertheless, as with the case of the DNA test, the patina tests conducted are based on suspicious samples, and the results, presented as virtually conclusive, turn out to be less than convincing.

Patina Testing

Patina testing was described in *The Jesus Family Tomb* as a method of analyzing mineral deposits, which built up on artifacts over years, to determine the archaeological origin, or provenance, of that artifact.

> "In theory, the patina inside a tomb or on the surfaces of its artifacts should develop its own chemically distinct signature, depending on a constellation of variable conditions, including the minerals and bacterial populations present at any specific location and the quantities of water moving through that specific 'constellation.' If such a chemical 'fingerprint' existed, scanning patina samples on a quantum level with an electron microprobe would reveal a chemical spectrum that could be matched to a specific tomb and to any objects that come from it."[179]

Questions arise, however, about the legitimacy of examining the patina of an ossuary that has no incontrovertible archaeological provenance, as well as a dubious history in the hands of perpetrators of antiquities fraud. A picture released by the IAA shows the ossuary resting on top of a toilet, thus casting further doubt on the condition of the artifact. Also, it was found that fraud had also been perpetrated with regard to the patina of the James ossuary and not simply the inscription.

---

[178] *The Lost Tomb of Jesus*, The Discovery Channel (2007)

[179] Simcha Jacobovici and Charles Pellegrino, *The Jesus Family Tomb* (2007) p. 176

> "Deputy director of the [IAA], [Geological Survey of Israel (GSI)] director Amos Bein [stated] that its representative to the IAA's committee established to determine the authenticity of the objects, Avner Ayalon, determined that the patina covering both the letters and surface of the . . . inscription on the James Ossuary, "could not have formed under natural climactic conditions . . . that prevailed in the Judea Mountains during the last 2000 years." Furthermore, the patina contained in the inscription on the James Ossuary is "significantly different from the oxygen isotopic composition in the surface patina of [the ossuary] and of patina of authentic ossuaries stored in [Jerusalem's] Rockefeller Museum." An internal GSI committee reviewed and approved Dr. Ayalon's conclusions."[180]

The tests that indicate forgery of the patina in the James ossuary inscription also cast doubt on the usefulness of any portion of the patina for determining the archaeological provenance of the ossuary. Further confirmation of the IAA findings was sought through independent testing of patina samples.

> "The patina of the James Ossuary inscription was tested independently by IAA scientific committee members Yuval Goren (micromorphology) and Ayalon (mass spectrometry). Both tests independently support the IAA's conclusion that . . . the inscription on the James Ossuary [is a forgery]."[181]

Dr. Ronny Reich, professor in the Department of Archaeology at Haifa University in Israel, is a scholar who agrees with the finding of fraud with regard to the James inscription patina.

> "Having some knowledge of geology, and in light of ['the results of the new geological study conducted by my friends Avner Ayalon from the Geological Survey of Israel and Professor Yuval Goren of Tel Aviv University'], I must note that I am now convinced that the patina we have seen was produced and placed inside the letters in an artificial manner and could not have been produced in nature in ancient times."[182]

Furthermore, former IAA Senior Curator of Archaeology and Anthropology Joe Zias has questioned the choice of personnel for patina analysis in *The Lost Tomb of Jesus*. He suggests that a professional with more expertise in materials specifically from

---

[180] Kristen Romey, "Geologists: Ossuary Patina Faked," http://www.archaeology.org/online/news/patina.html (June 23, 2003)

[181] *Ibid.*

[182] Amos Kloner and Ronny Reich, "The 'James son of Joseph' Ossuary," http://www.bibleinterp.com/articles/Kloner_Reich_report.htm (2000)

Israel and in the geological processes associated with patina formation would have been more appropriate.

> "This is a natural geological process which occurs over time. The forensic people involved in this segment have no experience whatsoever with local materials, in fact, one of the specialists' forte is in automobile crashes of which I'm sure he is very capable. There was one Israeli involved in this, behind the scenes, who was asked to obtain patina samples for the show. Sometime earlier, he pronounced a metal sheeting found at Qumran which he authenticated as ancient for a NOVA documentary. Within 12 months, the 2,000 year old object was found to have been painted with Barium-Titanium paint, patented in the 1920's to prevent oxidization. Watching this pseudo-science analysis reminds one more of a train wreck than a car crash."[183]

In a published electronic correspondence, Zias, with a sarcastic tone, further questions the choice of personnel for patina testing as well as the usefulness of the test presented in the documentary.

> "The US lab which ran some of these tests specializes in such things as car homicides [and] run of the mill forensic issues and have nothing whatsoever to do with archaeology. [Also,] had they sampled other patinas in other collections they would have found that all ossuaries found in Jerusalem basically would share the same geological features, [the] same time period, [and the] same stone."[184]

Thus, in light of the fraud-laden history of the ossuary, the suspicious patina, and the choice of personnel for conducting the tests, the usefulness of patina testing in providing informative results is highly suspect.

Measurements

According to James D. Tabor in *The Lost Tomb of Jesus*, the dimensions of the James ossuary are the same as those of the supposed missing ossuary from the Talpiot tomb.

> "I checked the dimensions... the dimensions of [the missing] ossuary are the same as the James ossuary."[185]

---

[183] Joe Zias, "[Viewer's] guide to the Talpiot Tomb documentary," http://www.joezias.com/tomb.html

[184] Darrell L. Bock, "Joseph Zias on the 10th Ossuary and the James Ossuary," http://dev.bible.org/bock/node/136 (March 20, 2003)

[185] *The Lost Tomb of Jesus*, The Discovery Channel (2007)

In spite of this unqualified statement that the measurements of the two ossuaries in question are the same, a passage in the conclusion of *The Jesus Family Tomb* raises suspicion.

> "According to Amos Kloner's report, IAA ossuary 80/509 – the missing ossuary – is 30 centimeters high. The James ossuary is 30.2 centimeters high. Ossuary 80/509 is 26 centimeters wide. The James ossuary is 26 centimeters wide. Finally, the missing ossuary is 60 centimeters in length. The James ossuary is 56.5 centimeters in length, a 3.5-centimeter discrepancy."[186]

No mention of this discrepancy was made by Tabor in the documentary. Nevertheless, the authors of the book suggest possible reasons for the difference in measured length.

> "It's possible, as has been suggested, that, because the James ossuary broke en route to Toronto and was then reglued, its original length changed slightly. But we don't even have to go this route. Given the preliminary nature of the inspection and the fact that the numbers of the missing ossuary are rounded to even numbers across the board, it may very well be that the initial measurements are off by 3.5 centimeters on one side. So, the missing ossuary and the James ossuary may be one and the same after all."[187]

To their credit, the authors do not pursue the possibility of a lengthening of the dimensions resulting from gluing a crack. It is highly implausible that a crack in a material would require 3.5 centimeters (almost 1.5 inches) of glue. Furthermore, such a wide crack in a rigid material like stone, which is likely brittle, would probably result in a complete splitting of the artifact into two or more pieces, possibly with further damage throughout. Such could not really be referred to as simply a 'crack.'

The explanation proffered as most plausible in this case is that of mistaken measurement. A look at Kloner's report in *Atiquot* reveals that the measurements were given in increments of 0.5 centimeters, not whole number increments. Furthermore, one must question why two out of three measurements taken by Kloner, which are apparently within 0.2 centimeters of the corresponding James ossuary measurements in each case (much less than the 0.5 centimeter measurement increment), are considered trustworthy, while the third measurement, off by a staggering 3.5 centimeters, is

---

[186] Simcha Jacobovici and Charles Pellegrino, *The Jesus Family Tomb* (2007) p. 210
[187] *Ibid.*

written off as an 'initial' measurement. Correspondingly, the reader is apparently expected to conclude that an initial or preliminary measurement is sloppy and may therefore be expected to occasionally have an error of at least 3.5 centimeters.

Human errors do indeed occur, and measurements may be made in error as the result of a number of factors. Nevertheless, it is yet another case of special pleading to assert that the measurement recorded by Kloner must have a drastic error simply because it does not match with the James ossuary. An error of 3.5 centimeters, or about 1.5 inches, is not a small mistake that can easily be written off as random error. It must be either sloppiness or intentional deception on the part of the archaeologist.

Placing blame for this discrepancy on measurement error could be justified more convincingly by way of finding other similar measurement errors in the case of other ossuaries. No such evidence is presented, however. Thus, the fact that a discrepancy in the measurements exists, even though this was not mentioned in the documentary, suggests that the James ossuary and the supposed missing Talpiot ossuary are not the same.

Photos of the James Ossuary

Further evidence against the notion that the James ossuary is from the Talpiot tomb is found in pictures of the James ossuary taken by Oded Golan. The photographs were dated 1976. If this date is accurate, or even nearly accurate, to within a few years, then the James ossuary cannot be from the Talpiot tomb, which was first unearthed in 1980.

To buttress the claim that the James ossuary belongs to the tomb, the claim that the photographs of the James ossuary were taken before the tomb's discovery must be discounted. Once again, as with the measurements of the ossuaries, a mistake or deception must be assumed to support the case.

> "Oded Golan, owner of the James ossuary, has a black-and-white picture of his ossuary, dating back to the time when he claims he bought it. The photograph was sent to a Washington, D.C. lab that determined that it had not been doctored and that it was printed on Kodak paper that was discontinued in 1980, the exact year of the Talpiot discovery."[188]

---

[188] *Ibid.*

Little further justification for discounting the photograph is given. Granted, the photograph was in the hands of a suspected swindler, and therefore independent confirmation was sought. Nevertheless, no evidence was presented that, in this case, fraud was perpetrated.

Gerald Richards, a respected retired special agent with the Federal Bureau of Investigation (FBI) and former forensics examiner with the FBI Laboratories Document Section, was called by Golan's defense as an expert witness. Richards, who also formerly served as chief of the Special Photographic Unit in the FBI, confirmed that there was no evidence to suggest tampering or falsification of the printed date on the photographs.

> "In the defense's photographs, dated 1976, the ossuary is shown on a shelf, apparently in Golan's home. In an enlargement, the whole inscription can be seen with great difficulty. The photo was examined by Gerald Richard, a former FBI agent and an expert for the defense. Richard testified that 'Nothing was noted that would indicate or suggest that they were not produced in March 1976 as indicated on the stamps appearing on the reverse side of each print.' Golan's attorney, Lior Beringer, told [Ha'aretz] that the photos support the defense's position. 'The prosecution claims that Golan forged the inscription after the beginning of 2000. But here is a detailed report from an FBI photo lab that states that the inscription existed at least since the 70s,' Beringer said."[189]

Correspondence with the FBI indicated that Gerald Richards did, indeed, examine the photograph in question.

> "The photo was examined by Gerald Richards of Richards Forensic Services."[190]

Based on the available evidence, then, there is no reason to suspect that the date on the photograph was altered. While there may be suspicion due to Golan's indictment for antiquities fraud, the photograph may not be simply dismissed without further evidence. This is the same approach taken by Tabor, who cites the supposedly genuine portion of the James ossuary inscription.

> "A lot of people have concluded – experts – that the James ossuary is a forgery, but nobody says it's all a forgery. And the position now of the Israel Antiquities

---

[189] Amiram Barkat, "Collector accused of forging 'James ossuary' says old photos prove authenticity," http://www.haaretz.com/hasen/spages/823215.html (February 9, 2007)

[190] E-mail correspondence with Special Agent Ann Todd, Public Affairs, FBI Laboratory (March 30, 2007)

Chapter Ten: 7th claim - The James Ossuary

> Authority is that it originally said 'James son of Joseph.'"[191]

Furthermore, following the reasoning of Simcha Jacobovici, since the evidence was admitted into court during the trial of Golan, there must be some significance or value to it.

> "[The patina test results] has now been introduced in – this week – in the ongoing case of the James ossuary forgery and will be introduced as evidence in Israel, in Jerusalem, in that ongoing trial.... It means that it's strong enough to be accepted as evidence."[192]

The insinuation made here by Jacobovici is that the patina tests have some additional value or credibility due to their admission into a court of law. By this logic, however, the same standard must be applied to the expert testimony with regard to the photographs of the James ossuary. Whatever the results of the patina tests, the photographs, if genuine, raise an irreconcilable difficulty for any association of the James ossuary with the Talpiot tomb.

The Tenth Ossuary: Missing or Discarded?

For an ossuary from the Talpiot tomb to have ended up in the hands of Oded Golan, it must have been stolen or otherwise lost by the IAA. This is the assertion of *The Lost Tomb of Jesus*, based partly on the testimony of archaeologist Shimon Gibson.

> "I went to the storerooms of the Israel Antiquities Authority in Bet Shemesh. They provided me with this computer [printout] which indicates that from this tomb there are nine items.... And it has the description of these ossuaries and where they are located in the storerooms."[193]

In his 1996 report in *Atiquot* summarizing the findings from 1980, Kloner testified that the tenth ossuary did not go missing, but had been discarded.

> "Due to a lack of storage space, only nine of the 10 ossuaries found in the tomb in 1980 were held by the Israel Antiquities Authority after they were

---

[191] *The Lost Tomb of Jesus*, The Discovery Channel (2007)

[192] Ted Koppel, "The Lost Tomb of Jesus: A Critical Look," The Discovery Channel (March 4, 2007)

[193] *The Lost Tomb of Jesus*, The Discovery Channel (2007)

> examined and documented. But the tenth one that was discarded did not have any inscription."[194]

This statement is in accord with the report, which lists the controversial ossuary 80.509 as 'plain.' Zias also attests to this observation.

> "[Kloner and others] would have noticed any ossuary with an inscription, particularly since the 'James ossuary" was decorated with two rosettes on the front, traces of red paint and an inscription on the reverse. . . . The 10th ossuary fell into the category of discard. . . . Tabor knew this as he was told by myself personally well in advance of the [documentary]."[195]

This consideration raises a further difficulty: if the James ossuary is the same as ossuary 80.509, Kloner must once again be suspected of committing sloppy or incompetent work, or he must be suspected of deception. The *Atiquot* report makes no mention of an inscription *Ya'akov bar Yehosef.* Since it is the assertion of Tabor, and others involved with *The Jesus Family Tomb* project, that this portion of the inscription is genuine, an irreconcilable discrepancy has been reached. Once more, the evidence proffered by the authors relies upon implicit accusations of deception or incompetence on the part of professional archaeologists.

The frequent reliance upon this type of insinuation would seem to fit with the general conspiratorial tone of the book, which suggests, either implicitly or explicitly, that people such as the Gospel writer Matthew, Jesus of Nazareth, and archaeologist Amos Kloner have either held secrets or lied outright. Without further evidence, however, accusations of this type are not credible.

Conclusion

The James ossuary, like so many other purported pieces of evidence in this case, falls short. The need for far too many conspiratorial cases of incompetence or deception, along with the required dismissal of evidence such as photographs and incongruous measurements, stretches the credibility of any

---

[194] Julie Stahl, "'Jesus Tomb' Filmmakers Should Be Ashamed, Archeologist Says," http://www.cnsnews.com/news/viewstory.asp?Page=/ForeignBureaus/archive/200703/INT20070301a.html (March 1, 2007)

[195] Darrell L. Bock, "Joseph Zias on the 10th Ossuary and the James Ossuary," http://dev.bible.org/bock/node/136 (March 20, 2007)

objective reasoner. Therefore, yet another of the key claims of *The Jesus Family Tomb* must be discarded as unwarranted. In spite of the utter lack of evidence that suggests that the conclusion of the authors is incorrect, one further claim remains to be debunked.

James Ossuary Throne
(Source: Israel Antiquities Authority)

Before the James ossuary was displayed across the world as the ossuary that could change history, it was originally stored in the most advanced antiquities facility in the world…Mr. Golan's toilet.

STUDY QUESTIONS:

1. Explain why the James ossuary patina testing is problematic.

2. Explain why the filmmakers claim the 10th ossuary was missing even though the original curator (Joe Zias) told them it wasn't.

3. If an FBI photo forensics expert was able to date a photo of the James ossuary to 1976, why do the filmmakers continue to assert that the James ossuary was from the 1980 Talpiot tomb?

4. Why are the first hand testimonies of Joe Zias and Amos Koner plus the testimony of an FBI photo forensics expert ignored for a conspiracy theory?

eighth claim: reliability of the New Testament

> *"The Gospels as we know them today have been retranscribed and rewritten many times and translated from one language to another...with corresponding losses in nuanced meaning. They have been edited by Church fathers . . . to conform to their subsequent vision of orthodoxy."*
> -James Cameron

Perhaps the most disturbing inconsistency in *The Lost Tomb of Jesus* and *The Jesus Family Tomb* is the selective reliance on New Testament scriptures. While, at some points, relying on certain portions of the accounts of the Gospels of Matthew, Mark, Luke, and John, the authors simultaneously ignore other portions. This approach is not necessarily unjustified, as it is conceivable that a given text may have evidence for reliability at some points and a lack of such evidence at other points. Consistency, however, is the proper measure in dealing with partially accepted texts.

A very questionable approach to New Testament scripture is revealed in *The Lost Tomb of Jesus* when the story of the woman caught in the act of adultery is related.

> "One of the most famous [stories] associated with Mary Magdalene is in the Gospel of John, where Jesus stops the stoning of a woman punished for adultery."[196]

Regardless of whether this text is truly about Mary Magdalene, the factual inaccuracy of this statement is disturbing.

---

[196] *The Lost Tomb of Jesus*, The Discovery Channel (2007)

Chapter Eleven: 8th claim – Reliability of the New Testament

As the narrator of the documentary speaks, a dramatization is shown that depicts a woman being pummeled with stones by a number of men. Her bloody countenance is revealed after Jesus steps in and stops the stoning. The biblical rendition of the story, however, is different.

> "Then the scribes and Pharisees brought to [Jesus] a woman caught in adultery. And when they had set her in the midst, they said to Him, 'Teacher, this woman was caught in adultery, in the very act. Now Moses, in the law, commanded us that such should be stoned. But what do You say?' ... [Jesus] said to them, 'He who is without sin among you, let him throw a stone at her first.' ... Then those who heard it... went out ... And Jesus was left alone, and the woman standing in the midst."[197]

Far from depicting Jesus as a passerby who breaks up a stoning in progress, it is instead presented in the New Testament text as a stoning that never took place. Interestingly, one of the most common mantras of the current culture involves the statement, "Let he who has no sin cast the first stone." Nevertheless, the portrayal in the documentary fails to recognize the content of a common cultural moralism and inaccurately represents the biblical event.

This inaccuracy, although it has no direct bearing on the hypothesis of *The Jesus Family Tomb*, is nonetheless troublesome for its sloppy handling of a text that is, ultimately, heavily relied upon for information. Such a careless error reveals either laziness in reading the actual text or intentional misrepresentation of the content of the text. Admittedly, the portrayal of Jesus breaking up a stoning is much more entertaining than that of Jesus dialoging with the scribes and Pharisees over a matter of law, but there are other opportunities for entertainment in this documentary that do not require inaccurate representation of the text of the New Testament.

---

[197] John 8:3-9 (NKJV)

Reliability of the New Testament

James Cameron, in his foreword to *The Jesus Family Tomb*, casts doubt upon the reliability and historical authenticity of the Gospels.

> "The Gospels as we know them today have been retranscribed and rewritten many times and translated from one language to another – from Aramaic to Greek to Coptic to Latin to various forms of English – with corresponding losses in nuanced meaning. They have been edited by Church fathers, centuries after the original words were spoken, to conform to their subsequent vision of orthodoxy."[198]

This statement by Cameron conveys the notion that the New Testament texts were translated from one language to another sequentially, a process that would, indeed, very likely result in loss or addition of nuanced meaning. This is not the way the texts are treated, however. Cameron is not the only individual in the world to have realized that a proper understanding of a text requires a proper understanding of the original language and culture. Furthermore, many scholars believe that the original texts are either available or can be reconstructed in a rational manner through textual criticism. One such scholar is James Malcolm Arlandson, professor of philosophy and world religion at Southern California College in Costa Mesa. He suggests that the kind of critical eye cast upon the New Testament texts is both unwarranted and inconsistent, as many other ancient texts are accepted as accurate with little dispute.

> "We may not have the original books and letters of the New Testament (and no text today coming from the ancient world has the originals), but we can reconstruct it as accurately as possible in our present state of knowledge. If we consider Greco-Roman classics as accurate, though they do not have as many manuscripts so soon after the originals, then why not accept the New Testament as accurate?"[199]

Additionally, the late Dr. Bruce M. Metzger, former George L. Collord Professor of New Testament Language and Literature at

---

[198] Simcha Jacobovici and Charles Pellegrino, *The Jesus Family Tomb* (2007) p. x

[199] James Arlandson, "The Manuscripts Tell the Story: The New Testament Is Reliable," http://www.americanthinker.com/2007/03/the_manuscripts_tell_the_story.html (March 3, 2007)

Princeton Theological Seminary, who was also described in an article at the Society of Biblical Literature (SBL) website as "internationally renowned textual critic, bible scholar, and biblical translator,"[200] commends the reliability and very early extant sources of the New Testament.

> "In contrast with these figures [about non-Christian Roman writers], the textual critic of the New Testament is embarrassed by the wealth of material. Furthermore, the work of many ancient authors has been preserved only in manuscripts that date from the Middle Ages (sometimes the late Middle Ages), far removed from the time at which they lived and wrote. On the contrary, the time between the composition of the books of the New Testament and the earliest extant [existing] copies is relatively brief... several papyrus manuscripts of portions of the New Testament are extant that were copied within a century or so after the composition of the original documents."[201]

According to Lee Strobel, Metzger believed that the available ancient texts for the New Testament were far more numerous than other writings that were otherwise believed to be accurate.

> "Dr. Metzger considers other ancient literary works for comparison. For instance, the first century Josephus is considered a trustworthy source for Jewish history. His widely accepted work The Jewish War has about nine manuscripts written in the tenth, eleventh, and twelfth centuries. There's one Latin manuscript in the fourth century. On another example, Homer's popular work Iliad has about 650 Greek manuscripts. The New Testament in contrast, has over 5,000 Greek manuscripts catalogued. There are about 8,000 to 10,000 Latin manuscripts, 8,000 in Ethiopic, Slavic, and Armenian. All of which combined are about 99.5% pure – more so than any work in antiquity. He says even if the Greek manuscripts are removed, the New Testament would still exist."[202]

Cameron also states in *The Jesus Family Tomb* that there is doubt among many experts regarding the historicity of Jesus and that he may have been concocted based on pagan stories of the death and resurrection of god-men that predate the time of Jesus' purported existence.

---

[200] Michael W. Holmes, "Dr. Bruce Manning Metzger 1914-2007," http://www.sbl-site.org/Article.aspx?ArticleId=638 (2007)

[201] James Arlandson, "The Manuscripts Tell the Story: The New Testament Is Reliable," http://www.americanthinker.com/2007/03/the_manuscripts_tell_the_story.html (March 3, 2007)

[202] Lee Strobel, *The Case for Christ*, Zondervan (1998)

> "What if Jesus didn't exist at all? Today many experts are saying exactly that. The theory is that he was a conflation of pagan god-man and death/Resurrection myths with first-century Jewish messiah traditions and that he had no more historical substance than Zeus. In various pagan mystery religions predating the first century [A.D.], Osiris, Attis, and Dionysus were all god-men who died around the time of Easter (the spring equinox) and were resurrected after three days. And all three of these deities predated Jesus by centuries."[203]

One might be curious to see the list of ostensible experts that Cameron marshals to the cause of denying Jesus' historical existence. Regardless of the number of proponents of such a minority view, Dr. Gary R. Habermas, Distinguished Professor and Chair of the Department of Philosophy and Theology at Liberty University, contradicts such a claim.

> "Let's take Adonis. Adonis is probably the ancient god for which we have the clearest data that he was raised from the dead. We have four accounts that Adonis was raised, the earliest one is the second century A.D., the other ones are between the second century and fourth century A.D. The earliest account we have for Attis is a third century A.D., and while Isis and Osiris as a religion was definitely pre-Christian, there was no resurrection in Isis and Osiris. Osiris in particular was not raised . . . Dionyus, I don't know [any scholar] who thinks Dionyus is pre-Christian: not the resurrection portion."[204]

Thus, the foreword of *The Jesus Family Tomb* presents a number of claims about the New Testament texts and the person of Jesus Christ that are extremely dubious. Perhaps most ironic is that, in later chapters of *The Jesus Family Tomb*, Jacobovici contradicts Cameron's statements that the Gospels are "our only record of the life and times of Jesus" and that Jesus' historical existence is doubtful.

> "[Jews] do believe that [Jesus] existed as a historical figure. The Talmud confirms this, and Josephus, in at least one line referring to [Jesus'] brother, also confirms this. So he existed."[205]

Historicity of Jesus

---

[203] *Ibid.*

[204] "Faith Under Fire" debate between Gary R. Habermas and Tim Callahan

[205] Simcha Jacobovici and Charles Pellegrino, *The Jesus Family Tomb* (2007) p. 137

Cameron's suggestion that Jesus' historical existence was doubtful until their "discovery" is a demonstration of what happens when a man who is totally incompetent about a certain field assumes he can be an authority. It's a vivid reminder of a Holiday Inn commercial where a stranger suddenly feels authoritative to join the ranks of experts studying a highly contagious virus just because he stayed at Holiday Inn (or in this case, Hollywood).

It doesn't take faith to realize the historicity of Jesus. Even our historical chronology such as the designations B.C. (Before Christ) and A.D. (Anno Domini, Latin for In the year of [Our] Lord) is a testament to His existence.

Additionally, there are extra biblical sources for Jesus. Ten non-Christian writers who lived within 150 years of Jesus' life mention His names, in contrast, only nine non-Christian writers mention Tiberius Caesar, who was the Roman Emperor at the time of Jesus.[206]

The non-Christian Jewish historian Josephus cited earlier, for example, narrates:

> "At this time [the time of Pilate] there was a wise man who was called Jesus. His conduct was good and [he] was known to be virtuous. And many people from among the Jews and the other nations became his disciples. Pilate condemned him to die...They reported that he had appeared to them after his crucifixion, and that he was alive; accordingly he was perhaps the Messiah, concerning whom the prophets have recounted wonders."[207]

Selective Use of New Testament Texts

The New Testament is cited throughout the book and documentary as a source of information. That information is used to determine the names of Jesus' family members, to describe key events in the lives of various characters, and to glean other facts vital to building evidence for the hypothesis. It is the selective use of these texts that is problematic.

---

[206] Geisler and Turek, p222.

[207] Antiquities of the Jews (A.D. 93) book 18, ch 3, sec 3.

In addressing the incongruous presence of the *Matya* ossuary, the genealogy of Mary is cited, with its numerous 'Matthews.' This is curious, especially since the text is, according to James Cameron, so unreliable. Furthermore, the use of the name *Yose* as a name for one of Jesus' brothers, as mentioned in Mark 6:3, is also inconsistent with the general atmosphere of mistrust painted by Cameron.

Another curiously selective use of the text involves the scene in the Gospel of John where Jesus is on the cross and speaks to Mary and the beloved disciple. Interestingly, the text is trusted in so far as a "beloved disciple" is mentioned, likely to support the hypothesis, which includes Jesus' begetting of a son, *Yehuda*. In *The Lost Tomb of Jesus*, the narrator suggests that the scene at Jesus' crucifixion points to a family relationship between Jesus, Mary Magdalene, and the beloved disciple.

> "In John 19:26, Jesus asks the beloved disciple at the base of the cross to behold his mother. He then says to Mary, 'Woman, behold your son.' Traditionally, this scene has been understood as Jesus addressing Mary, his mother. But can this be later theology? Could it be that Jesus was talking to Mary Magdalene, his wife, asking her to protect their son?"[208]

Aside from the fact that, according to this suggestion, it was required that a man dying an excruciating death on a cross would have been spending what precious little breath he had remaining in stating the obvious to the two onlookers, this statement ignores the text. Calling it a 'traditional' understanding and, possibly, "later theology," the narrator never mentions the obvious: John 19:26 states, "When Jesus saw His mother, and the disciple whom He loved standing by, He said to His mother, 'Woman, behold your son!'"

Failure to mention that it was not simply tradition, but the text itself, that identifies the woman Jesus' mother is a gratuitous omission. This represents a prime example of the attempt to "have it both ways" by using the New Testament texts as support for the hypothesis while simultaneously contradicting the texts. In this case, a single sentence was both cited and contradicted in the same breath, a classic case of unbridled bias and a far cry from a scholarly documentary.

---

[208] *The Lost Tomb of Jesus*, The Discovery Channel (2007)

Such rubber-stamping of New Testament (and other) texts is rampant in the book and the documentary. This is, disappointingly, yet another example of fallacious special pleading. No justification is presented for trusting certain texts over others; rather, those texts that support the presumed conclusion are accepted, and those texts that contradict it are dismissed. This presents an almost insurmountable difficulty, as the complete dismissal of the New Testament texts leaves a tremendous gap in the arguments of the authors. Yet, the complete acceptance of the New Testament texts requires acceptance of a chronicle of events that leaves no room for the notion that Jesus was buried in a tomb in East Talpiot, Israel.

Conclusion

With this revelation of the disingenuous and fallacious use of New Testament Scriptures, the major claims cited in this discussion have been shown to be faulty, unwarranted, or unacceptable cases of special pleading. Indeed, according to many scholars of textual criticism, the New Testament texts are extremely accurate and are based on many more manuscripts than are other ancient texts. It is only a minority view, contrary to any implications by James Cameron, that Jesus never existed or that the New Testament has been corrupted. In fact, it is believed by the majority of scholars, including those who have no sympathy for Christianity, that Jesus Christ was a historical man and that the New Testament has been transmitted through history in a very pure and uncorrupted form.

It remains only to review where the hypothesis of *The Lost Tomb of Jesus* and *The Jesus Family Tomb* stands in light of the devastating paucity of evidence.

Erasmus, The Scholar
(Source: Holbein d. J., Hans)

STUDY QUESTIONS:

1. In the documentary, the filmmakers consider the gospels' empty tomb account as a lie but then use the gospels freely for the rest of their assumptions. What logical fallacy is this?

2. Cameron claims that demi-gods in antiquity have resurrection stories that predate Jesus. However, there were no written records of these stories until after Christ. Name the possible reasons why Cameron didn't mention this inconvenient fact.

12

conclusion

"If there is no resurrection of the dead, then Christ is not risen. And if Christ is not risen, then our preaching is empty and your faith is also empty."
-The Apostle Paul

What at first appeared to be a convincing case, with staggering odds in its favor, that an accidentally uncovered tomb in East Talpiot, Israel, belonged to Jesus Christ and His family has turned out to be nothing more than a speculative conjecture based on little or no evidence. What might have been viewed as a powerful threat to the faith of millions, if not billions, has proven to be nothing more than a paper tiger.

Orthodox Christianity proclaims that the crucified Jesus Christ rose from the grave and ascended, bodily, into heaven. Not only does the attempt of a few men to contradict this proclamation fall in the face of extensive testimony from scholars, many of whom are non-Christians, but it also falls in the face of two thousand years of history.

Claims Reviewed

In examining where the hypothesis of *The Jesus Family Tomb* and *The Lost Tomb of Jesus* now stand, it is helpful to review the major claims of the authors, along with the response of both scholars and simple reasoning.

- The Talpiot tomb discovery went unreported.

Citation of numerous scholarly and popular publications, most of them written as early as a decade or more before publication of *The Jesus Family Tomb*, indicates that this dilute claim is patently false. Even a BBC documentary, which was not mentioned in the *The Lost Tomb of Jesus* documentary discussed the Talpiot tomb and its possible connection with Jesus Christ.

- The controversial inscriptions are to be read *Yeshua bar Yehosef* and *Mariamene e Mara*.

While these may be possible readings of the inscriptions, they are by no means the consensus readings. The number of additional markings in the *Yeshua* inscription makes deciphering the word difficult, as attested by Kloner, Rahmani, and others. Questions also abound with regard to the reading of *Mariamene e Mara*, which is believed by Pfann to be *Mariame kai Mara* instead. Regardless of the true readings, they are not as clear as was suggested in *The Jesus Family Tomb*.

- Jesus and his family were buried in Jerusalem.

There's little biblical testimony that exists that supports the claim that the Talpiot tomb is the final resting place for Jesus' family. Thus, numerous speculative claims were proffered in an attempt to justify the notion that Yose, Mary, Matthew, and, not to mention, Jesus were all buried in Jerusalem. Additionally, it was found to be little more than speculation that the names inscribed on the ossuaries were related in the same way as the family of Jesus, as witnessed by the Bible or other ancient texts. The authors also conveniently ignored origins, where the name of the hometown is inscribed if they are not from the area. For example, Jesus of Nazareth or Mary of Magdalene.

- Mariamne, or *Mariamene*, is Mary Magdalene.

In attempting to defend the claim, which was shown to be based on circular reasoning, the authors of *The Jesus Family Tomb* begin to display patent bias and deceptive tactics, especially when presenting the testimony of Bovon. Bovon's claims regarding the Acts of Philip, a non-contemporaneous text, include the possible literary identification of the character Mariamne with Mary

Magdalene. The authors turn this tentative suggestion into a historical identification that goes beyond the limits of Bovon's words. In the end, *The Jesus Family Tomb* merely begs the question by asserting that the *Mariamene* of the ossuary is the Mary Magdalene of history.

The authors preferred to use an embellished apocryphal book as their authority over eyewitness testimony of people who witnessed Jesus' final days. It's like using Iran as the authoritative source on the Holocaust instead of the Jews who actually witnessed it.

- Statistical analysis supports the claim that the tomb is that of Jesus and his family.

After examination of the assumptions that go into the analysis and demonstration that the assumptions are far from accurate, it is found that the numbers are meaningless and does not lend credence to the hypothesis of *The Jesus Family Tomb*. On the contrary, it is highly likely that a more accurate statistical analysis would show that the tomb is almost certainly not that of Jesus.

- DNA tests prove that Jesus and Mary Magdalene were married.

Ignoring the fact that it was never proven that Jesus and Mary Magdalene were ever interred in the Talpiot tomb, the DNA tests, in fact, prove almost nothing. With problems ranging from the integrity of the DNA in the samples, the questionable source of the samples, and the less than informative results, little was gained from these tests. Indeed, it was shown that there was no maternal relationship between the sources from whom the DNA samples were obtained. Nevertheless, despite the mysterious identities of the sources, a lack of maternal relationship still leaves numerous other possibilities. The two individuals could have been half-brother and half-sister (assuming they were male and female), cousins, or any number of other relationships. There are also other possibilities such as contamination from vandals. The results of the

DNA analysis do little to convince a skeptical viewer or reader that relationship by marriage is the logical conclusion.

- The James ossuary was from the Talpiot tomb.

Although much was made of the James ossuary in both *The Jesus Family Tomb* and *The Lost Tomb of Jesus*, it was found, upon closer examination, that little evidence supported this claim. The seldom-mentioned disparity in dimensions of the ossuaries and the fact that the James ossuary was found to be a forgery by the IAA and independent bodies, shatter any credibility to the hypothesis that this was the tomb of Jesus of Nazareth and his brother, James. The authors only succeeded in showing their own biases and preconceived opinions.

- The New Testament is an unreliable text.

Throughout *The Jesus Family Tomb*, the authors made it clear that they could not decide whether to accept or reject this claim. The bi-polar reliance upon the text for historical information in one breath and denial of its historical veracity in the next, reveals the unrelenting bias of the authors at the expense of truth. The New Testament was authoritative only when it helped establish their a priori conclusions which were already pre-packaged with their hypothesis, but discredited when it conflicted with those conclusions.

It was shown that the New Testament is highly reliable and has not been altered as James Cameron claims. His statements about the unreliability of the New Testament and the non-historicity of Jesus were based more on his freedom of speech to air his feelings towards Christianity than on evidence.

The Jesus Family Tomb: Is It Fact or Fiction?

In light of the foregoing examination of the claims by the authors, it becomes clear that they failed miserably to show any credible evidence that the east Talpiot tomb bore the remains of Jesus Christ and his family. In response to the question, "Is it fact or fiction?" the answer can only be a resounding '*Fiction.*'

Borrowing from Dr. Reed's words: "It's very exciting, it's stimulating…but deep down you know it's wrong."

Chapter Twelve: Conclusion

Jesus Ascension
(Source: Standard Pub Co)

epilogue

By Dr. Diego D. Sausa

Author of *Kippur The Final Judgment*

    What if God really does not exist? What if we're really all alone in this cold insuperable and infinite universe where the only thing that's permanent is eternal nothingness before and after us, and the only ultimate reality is our final destiny which is the grave; where all our achievements, endeavors, loves, knowledge, dreams, wealth and aspirations are sucked into eternal oblivion like a sparkling dew on a spire of grass vaporized by the heat of the morning sun? Then it wouldn't matter whether one believes in God or not. It wouldn't make any difference if one is a satisfied, "smart," staunch, atheist or a "blind," happy, faithful, self-sacrificing Christian. There's nothing to glory nor cheer about having the right world view nor reason to convince or chastise others for believing differently because everyone ends up a loser anyway no matter which side of the fence he/she belongs. Why all the hassle and the fuss about who's better when the inevitable denouement of everyone's passions, beliefs, convictions, knowledge, struggles and accomplishments is death?

    Wealth, status, love, success – none are immune to the worms' rapacious burrowings. Dreams (miracles too) don't escape their squirmy jaws. Even if our lives were bountiful, happy, fulfilled – an ascent from one triumph to another, from one joy to another – death leaves it all in a well-trimmed dump....[But] Most lives, though, are parsed, not into success, happiness, and fulfillment, but into tragedy, suffering and fear, which ends only when the brain stops getting oxygen....What a pathetic existence, when the only sure remedy for pain, fear, and sorrow is cerebral suffocation!....A common sadness pervades the species; a universal sigh hisses from its lips, as if squeezed out by gravity (or is something in the water?), even if the sound's muffled by the flat caws of crows or the tickle of brooms. Death alone mutes it. What a paradox: The only thing that ends pain causes so much of it![209]

    Man has finally come to a point where he has discovered the mysteries of omnipresent photons in the quantum realm, map out the DNA of the *homo sapiens*, and calculate the infinite precision

---

[209] Clifford Goldstein, *God, Gödel, and Grace* (Maryland: Review and Herald Publishing Assn., 2003), pp. 92-93.

that holds this vast universe together in place to allow life on this earth. With all the "isms" that our materialistic postmodern world has invented in place of a transcendent God, man has indeed come to a point where he seemingly has become "the measure of all things," and appears to have gotten closer to achieving his fundamental project which is, as existentialist atheist Jean-Paul Sartre describes, "the desire to be God."[210] And yet the greatest tragedy of it all is, despite all these accomplishments, and despite the fact that his brain is equivalent to 20 million volumes worth of information,[211] mankind hasn't found any meaning to his own existence (because without God there is none). It's only limitless nothingness before and limitless nothingness after his fleeting existence.

"I see the terrifying spaces of the universe hemming me in," says Blaise Pascal while exploring the mind that sees a God-less universe, "and I find myself attached to one corner of this vast expanse without knowing why I have been put in this place rather than that, or why the brief span of life allotted to me should be assigned to one moment rather than another of all the eternity which went before me and all that will come after me. I see only infinity on every side, hemming me in like an atom or like the shadow of a fleeting instant. All I know is that I must soon die, but what I know least about is this very death which I cannot evade."[212] Jewish atheist turned theologian and philosopher Clifford Goldstein vividly portrays this miserable plight of the postmodern *homo sapiens*:

> [S]tep by step man's ties to the transcendent…to a personal loving God, became unmoored until man found himself alone in a cold cosmic void, with truth only what he makes it….Yet by severing ties with the transcendent…man has come to the point where, if there is to be hope, it must be found in himself, in whatever values, truths, and meaning he can derive from existence through 'human reason and empirical observation' because there's nothing else above, no deity to reveal it to him. Humanity alone erects the pillars of justice; we alone name good and evil; we alone create rules; we alone determine values….We become, like Eve in Eden, our own gods….But we're not. We're

---

[210] Jean-Paul Sartre, *Being and Nothingness* (New York: Washington Square Press, 1956, p. 724.
[211] Carl Sagan, *Cosmos* (New York: Random House, 1980), p. 278.
[212] Blaise Pascal, *Pensées* (New York: Penguin Books, 1995), p. 130.

not even close, and, in fact, the harder we try to be like God the less like Him we become. We can be compared to people who – thinking they can get where they want to go by swimming rather than sailing – jump ship and, finding the water too deep and rough, cling only to each other in hope of staying afloat. We've rooted truth only in ourselves, and because we're weak, vacillating, fearful, evanescent, unstable, and sinking, our truths are weak, vacillating, fearful, evanescent, unstable, and sinking as well. By severing ourselves from God, man has only himself left, a prospect that…becomes increasingly depressing.…Modern secularism has brought us to an abyss as empty, unstable and shallow as the human ego.[213]

Deep in the innermost chamber of our souls is an intuitive cry for permanence, for consistency, for peace, security and perpetual happiness. And yet all that we see around us point to a bleak prospect of insecurity, terror, tragedy, death and total global extinction. Despite all the knowledge and advancements that mankind has achieved, he has come up with no answer to his certain doom. He can't even figure out how to stop a deranged man who steps into a classroom and starts shooting everyone. Nor can he figure out how that the *homo sapiens* who are supposed to get higher and higher in the evolutionary ladder, are getting worse and worse like untethered monsters. Mankind needs something that transcends himself to save him from his plight. Realizing this utter helplessness, Sartre laments: "It is very distressing that God does not exist, because all possibility of finding values in a heaven of ideas disappears along with Him…."[214]

What if our soul's intuitive desire for permanence, consistency, peace, security and eternal bliss is all because mankind had all these as normal realities of his seminal existence? What if by choice the first humans lost all these realities by default and an infinitely loving personal God exists who created the universe out of nothing; and though He rules the hundreds of billions of galaxies across the limitless space, He did not have second thoughts about coming down to this earth as one of us, and vicariously faced the wrath of His own infinite justice toward mankind's imperfection; and through His death and resurrection, He had made it possible for us to choose to get back to that

---

[213] Goldstein, *By His Stripes* (Idaho: Pacific Press Publishing Assn., 1999), pp. 20-22.

[214] Jean-Paul Sartre, *Existentialism and Human Emotions* (New York: Philosophical Library, 1957), p. 22.

utopian infinitude that we once had; because He created us to live (not die) forever? Atheist turned Christian, C.S. Lewis writes: "Creatures are not born with desires unless satisfaction of those desires exists. A baby feels hunger: well, there is such a thing as food. A duckling wants to swim: well, there is such a thing as water. Men feel sexual desire: well, there is such thing as sex. If I find in myself a desire which no experience in this world can satisfy, the most probable explanation is that I was made for another world."[215]

Sounds outlandish? Yes it does. But we need something outlandish to deliver us from our ultimate fate which is death. And without the answer to death, we can't have meaning to life either. We need to look for reality outside of empirical verification because the answer to death was given 2000 years ago, which is outside of empirical science. Do miracles happen? Did a supernatural event such as the resurrection of Jesus occur?

Modern empirical science precludes miracles because it's unnatural (it violates natural laws) and is unrepeatable. This modern thinking, the so-called Enlightenment (which threw away faith in God and was replaced by empirical science) is highly influenced by the Jewish pantheist Benedict Spinoza (1670s) and David Hume (1711-1776). Spinoza espoused that miracles were impossible because he believed that they violated natural laws which according to him were immutable.[216] Geisler and Turek rightly point out that such an assumption is flawed because natural laws are "descriptions" of what normally happens and not "prescriptions" of what should happen.[217] For example the law of gravity tells us that when a ball is tossed up, it falls to the ground and yet humans can stop the fall by catching the ball and thus overpower the law of gravity. And since humans can overpower natural laws, God in a grander sense, can likewise overpower nature.[218] Another flaw in Spinoza's reasoning is that it assumes that man knows all the natural laws and it assumes that he knows what is and what is not a violation of those laws. Is overpowering

---

[215] C.S. Lewis, *Mere Christianity* (New York: Simon and Schuster, 1996), p. 121.

[216] Norman L. Geisler and Frank Turek, *I Don't Have Enough Faith to Be an Atheist* (Illinois: Good News Publishers, 2004), pp. 203-204.

[217] Ibid., p. 204.

[218] Ibid.

the law of gravity such as catching a ball a violation of the natural law or a broader description of that law (i.e. when you catch the ball it stops the fall)? What if there are other natural laws that we don't know about (which certainly there are) that allow such occurrence? A good example of this is in the New Testament account of the Sabbath. The Sabbath is part of the Moral Law (The Ten Commandments) and is therefore, immutable. Christ Himself said that He did not come to destroy the Law but to fulfill (Matt. 5:17-19) because it's immutable (in fact He died because it's immutable, He had to vicariously meet the demands of His laws against the guilty mankind), and as His custom was (Mk. 1:21, Lk. 4:16) He went to the Synagogue on Sabbath day (and even the disciples long after Christ was gone, observed the Sabbath day as their day of rest and worship, Acts 13:14-16; 17:2, Heb. 4:9). And yet the Pharisees, with their limited understanding of the Sabbath, accused Christ of violating the Sabbath commandment when He healed people on the Sabbath day and allowed His disciples to eat corn on the same holy day. Christ rebuked the Pharisees by saying that He was Lord (the ultimate authority as to what was lawful to do and what was not on the Sabbath day) of the Sabbath and that it was lawful to help the sick and feed the hungry on the Sabbath day. He was arguing that helping the sick and feeding the hungry was contemplated by the Sabbath commandment and that doing such activities on the Sabbath day was actually part of keeping the Sabbath holy and not violating it (Lk. 6:1-9). The same is true when God performs a miracle, why should we assume that He is violating His natural laws? Do we know the laws of nature more than the One who made them? Knowing the eternal justice and consistency (He never changes) of God (He had to die rather than violate the demands of His own laws), we can conclude that God does not violate His own laws when He performs miracles. In fact, the greatest miracle of all (which Paul calls the mystery of Godliness) was when God came down to become a human and vicariously assumed the judgment that was ours according to the demands of His laws that we might have the eternal life that was His. In other words God performed the greatest miracle of saving us, by fulfilling the demands of His own law.

Another reason why modern science rejects miracles is largely due to David Hume's assumption that since a miracle by definition is a rare occurrence and has little evidence to support it compared to a regular occurrence which has much more evidence, therefore, a wise man should believe in regular or natural occurrences because of more evidence and not believe in miracles because they have less evidence.[219] The premise that normal occurrences that have more evidence are more believable compared to rare occurrences that have less evidence is fatally flawed. Geisler and Turek expose this fallacious reasoning: "There are many improbable (rare) events in life that we believe when we have good evidence for them....[W]e certainly don't tell a lottery winner who beat 76 million-to-one odds that he's not going to get his money until he can win it five times in a row! No, in these cases, the evidence for the rare is greater than that for the regular....So the issue is not whether an event is regular or rare – the issue is whether we have good evidence for the event."[220]

Is the miracle of the Resurrection possible? Of course! If we believe the evidence in modern science (the Big Bang) that our universe was created out of nothing (which points to an infinite Creator who performed this mind-boggling miracle), then one has to believe in the possibility of a lesser miracle such as the Resurrection. C.S. Lewis aptly says: "If we admit God, must we admit Miracle? Indeed, indeed, you have no security against it. That is the bargain."[221] In other words, in order to show that the Resurrection is not possible, one has to show that God's existence is not possible. And with all the modern scientific evidence that points to a supernatural God, it takes more faith to believe in the improbability of God than the probability of God. Do we have empirical evidence about the Resurrection? No we don't. Does reality reside within the confines of the empirical box? No it doesn't. Otherwise we might as well dismiss all beliefs about the beginning of the universe, the beginning of life, forensic science, history and archaeology because these are all unrepeatable events. And yet we know they are true because of the weight of valid evidence available to us. For examples, juries are able to come out with a guilty verdict beyond a reasonable doubt when the evidence points overwhelmingly to the criminal despite the fact that the actual crime is unrepeatable. Likewise we believe in the historicity of Plato, Alexander the Great, Napoleon and other historical

---

[219] Ibid., p. 205.

[220] Ibid., p. 207.

[221] Lewis, *Miracles* (New York: MacMillan, 1947), p. 106.

figures because of authentic testimonies and historical records about their existence.

Do we have sufficient authentic evidence for the historicity of Jesus Christ and the Resurrection? More than enough, but we will only consider the following: 1) First century historical accounts of non-Christian writers, 2) Eyewitness testimony, and, 3) Prophecy.

1ST CENTURY NON-CHRISTIAN ACCOUNT

Flavius Josephus (ca. 37-100), who became a Pharisee at the age of 19, began writing as a historian when he served under Roman emperor Domitian. He became known as the greatest Jewish historian of his time. In his work *Antiquities of the Jews* (XVIII, iii, 3) which he wrote in about 93 A.D., Josephus wrote the following account about Jesus:

Now there was about this time Jesus, a wise man, if it be lawful to call him a man, for he was a doer of wonderful works – a teacher of such men as receive the truth with pleasure. He drew over to him both many of the Jews, and many of the Gentiles. He was [the] Christ; and when Pilate, at the suggestion of the principal men amongst us, had condemned him to the cross, those that loved him at the first did not forsake him, for he appeared to them alive again the third day, as the divine prophets had foretold these ten thousand other wonderful things concerning him; and the tribe of Christians, so named from him, are not extinct at this day.[222]

There are ten known non-Christian sources that mention Jesus within 150 years of His life, three of those sources were considered anti-Christian, namely Celsus, Tacitus, and the Jewish Talmud. Within the same time frame, the number of sources that mention Tiberius Caesar, the emperor of Rome at the time of Christ was nine. From these ten non-Christian sources the following facts about Jesus are gleaned which agree with the New Testament account:

Jesus lived during the time of the Roman emperor Tiberius Caesar, He lived a virtuous life, He was a wonder-worker, He had a brother named James, He was acclaimed to be the Messiah, He was crucified under the Roman governor Pontius Pilate, He was

---

[222] *Josephus, The Complete Works*, William Whiston, translator (Nashville: Thomas Nelson Publishers, 1998), *Antiquities of the Jews*, XIII, iii, 3.

crucified on the eve of the Jewish Passover, darkness and an earthquake occurred when He died, His disciples believed that He rose from the dead, His disciples were willing to die for their belief, Christianity spread rapidly as far as Rome, and His disciples denied the Roman gods and worshiped Jesus as God.[223]

EYEWITNESS TESTIMONY

There were nine eyewitnesses to the resurrection who wrote down their testimony on 27 different scrolls which we now call the New Testament.[224] The question one would naturally posit is: Is the New Testament a reliable historical account? The answer to this question is a resounding yes, especially when we consider the following facts: (1) The time gap in years between the original writing and the first surviving copies found is 25 for the New Testament, 500 for Homer, 1,400 for Demosthenes, 1,400 for Herodotus, 1,200 for Plato, 1000 for Tacitus, 1000 for Caesar, and 750 for Pliny. Clearly the New Testament has the closest gap from the original document to the first surviving copy found; (2) The number of manuscript copies found for the New Testament original manuscripts is 5,686, for Homer is 643, for Herodotus is eight, for Plato is seven, for Tacitus is 20, for Caesar is ten and for Pliny is seven.[225] No other historical document comes close to the New Testament with regards to the number of supporting manuscripts found. Out of these 5,686 manuscript copies that were found the degree of accuracy of the copies is an outstanding 99.5 percent compared to Hinduisms *Mahabharata* which is 90 percent;[226] (3) The New Testament has been shown to meet the criteria used by historians to determine the authenticity of historical documents namely: (a) Is the testimony early, proximal to the event? (b) Is there an eyewitness testimony? (c) Is there multiple, independent eyewitness sources? (d) Are the eyewitnesses trustworthy? (e) Does archaeology corroborate the historical accounts? (f) Do opponents corroborate the account? (g) Does the

---

[223] Geisler and Turek, p. 223.

[224] Ibid., p. 224.

[225] Ibid., p. 226.

[226] Ibid.

testimony contain events or details that are embarrassing to the authors?[227]

The New Testament is an account of multiple independent actual eyewitnesses to the events surrounding Christ. When Peter and John were summoned by the Jewish authorities and were commanded to stop teaching in the name of Jesus they answered: "Judge for yourselves whether it is right in God's sight to obey you rather than God. For we cannot help speaking about what we have seen and heard" (Acts 4:18-20). Paul, a former persecutor of Christians turned apostle after his encounter with the risen Jesus on the road to Damascus, confirms that the twelve disciples and five hundred others saw the resurrected Christ (1 Cor. 15:4-8). The eyewitnesses who wrote the New Testament were trustworthy because they included details that were embarrassing to them particularly to their Master (e.g. Jesus was not believed by His own family, Jn. 7:5, was thought to be as a deceiver, Jn. 7:12), and also because archaeology and secular history corroborate the veracity of the characters and places that were described in their accounts. William Ramsay, a classical scholar and archaeologist, studied the book of Acts with initial skepticism, but after his study he said: "I began with a mind unfavorable to [Acts]....It did not lie then in my line of life to investigate the subject minutely; but more recently I found myself often brought into contact with the book of Acts as an authority for the topography, antiquities, and society of Asia Minor. It was gradually borne on me that in various details the narrative showed marvelous truth."[228]

Perhaps the most significant reason why the eyewitnesses were trustworthy is because none of them recanted his testimony about Jesus' resurrection even in the face of persecution and death. People may be willing to die for something they believe is true (although they may be wrong), and certainly there are people who would rather die than recant something that they know is true, but hardly is there anyone who would die for something that he knows is a lie. So the only plausible reason why none of Christ's disciples denied the resurrection in the face of losing everything including their own lives was because their testimony about Christ's resurrection was true.

---

[227] Ibid., pp. 252-324.

[228] William Ramsay, *St. Paul the Traveller and the Roman Citizen* (New York: Putnam, 1896), p. 8.

Chapter Twelve: Conclusion / Epilogue

PROPHECY

Jesus Himself declared that the reason for prophecy is to strengthen faith in God once the fulfillment of prophecy is manifested. He says "And now I have told you before it comes, that when it does come to pass, you may believe" (Jn. 14:29). That's one of the major factors that strengthened the faith of the disciples, when they saw the fulfillment of Christ's prophecy that He would die and rise again on the third day (Jn. 2:19-21). Perhaps the most amazing prophecy about the Messiah was made by Daniel who lived about 600 years before Christ. His prophecy that specifically points to the exact date of the coming of the Messiah (in Greek, Christos meaning Christ) is found in Daniel 9:24-27:

> Know therefore and understand that from the going forth of the command to restore and build Jerusalem until Messiah the Prince, there shall be seven weeks and sixty-two weeks…and after the sixty-two weeks [plus the prior seven weeks, thus 69 weeks] Messiah shall be cut off, but not for Himself…Then he shall confirm a covenant for many for one week; but in the middle of the week He shall bring an end to sacrifice and offering….

This prophecy commonly known as the seventy-week prophecy (which is actually made of 70 Sabbaths), not only gives the specific time for the advent of the Messiah but also the specific time for His death. Majority of scholars agree that the prophetic seventy weeks in Daniel 9 is weeks of years.[229] This is confirmed by Daniel's contemporary prophet Ezekiel who says that for God, a day is equivalent to a year (Ezek. 4:6). The above prophecy, therefore, gives us the following information: from the realization of the decree to restore and build Jerusalem (which was laid in ruins by the Babylonians) unto the Messiah the Prince shall be seven weeks and sixty-two weeks or a total of 69 weeks unto the Messiah the Prince. Translating 69 weeks (69 X 7) is 483 days and translating it into years is equal to 483 years. It's been established that the actualization of the decree to rebuild Jerusalem was in 457 BC, a Jewish sabbatical year.[230] The Jewish Talmud places a curse on those who try to calculate Daniel's Messianic prophecy

---

[229] Diego Sausa, *Kippur, The Final Judgment* (Florida: The Vision Press, 2006) p. 103.

[230] Ibid. p. 121-122.

understandably because 483 years after 457 BC brings us to A.D. 27, (another Jewish sabbatical year) and the New Testament records that on the "…fifteenth year…of Tiberius" (Luke 3:1) Jesus of Nazareth was anointed at His baptism and began His Messianic ministry. Daniel continues that "He shall confirm a covenant for many [technically all] for one week," that is in the last seven years of the 70-week prophecy, and "in the middle of the [70th] week, He shall bring an end to sacrifice and offering…." The middle of the last week (seven years) means three and a half years from the 69th week. Since the 69th week is in 27 AD, three and a half years after that would take us to around 31 A.D., Daniel says that the Messiah would bring an end to sacrifice and offering (sanctuary rituals). What happened in 31 A.D. that would bring and end to sanctuary sacrifices and offering? In that year Jesus Christ was crucified and the Bible records that when Christ "breathed His last," that very thick "veil of the temple" that separated the Most Holy Place from the Holy Place, "was torn in two from top to bottom" (Mark 15:38) signifying the end of symbolic sacrifices and offerings because the Real Offering and Sacrifice had been offered.

Of course the Jews fixed that very thick veil that was torn by an unseen "Hand" that separated the Holy Place from the Most Holy Place and continued to offer their offerings and sacrifices for 39 more years after Christ's crucifixion (until the temple was destroyed by the Romans in 70 A.D.). But in the eyes of God, those sacrifices were moot, the true Sacrifice had already been offered on the Cross, on a Friday afternoon as the Sabbath day (starts Friday sunset) was beginning, the Christ or the Messiah of the 70 Sabbaths, fully paid the ransom for the world's eternal salvation and divine rest – on a Sabbath day.[231]

Here is an unmistakable prophecy about Christ that gives the exact date of His Messiahship and His death, given in advance about 600 years before it happened. Christ Himself said that He gives us prophecy ahead of time as a sign for us to believe when it happens. If this very vivid sign of the supernatural doesn't make anyone believe, nothing will; or maybe there is, as one former atheist writes:

> Maybe, then, the best reason to accept isn't that of Christ's fulfillment of the Old Testament prophecies such as Daniel 9:24-27, in which six centuries before His birth the date

---

[231] Ibid. p. 124.

of His sacrifice was predicted with supernatural accuracy, but that without something to unearth the grave and undo death, our lives are off-key odes to meaninglessness, with nothing – not an echo, even – to show for all the preceding racket.

Or maybe the best reason is not that Jesus fulfilled the prophecy of Isaiah 53, which depicted His life and sacrifice more than 700 years before that life and sacrifice, but that deep down a hunger for something gnaws at us no matter how bloated our bellies or stroked our egos. Whatever we do, whatever triumphs we enjoy, and within whatever satisfactions our souls and senses luxuriate, a witching emptiness – an inexplicable angst – blunts every pleasure until every pleasure aches and nothing can heal those dull throbs except death (or God).

The historicity of Jesus, the evidence for His resurrection, or the testimony of the apostles, who lost all things for Christ, are not the best reasons for belief either. A better reason to believe is our need to believe, and a better reason to seek transcendence is our need for transcendence.

…How sad to be captured and commandeered by what's so small, so fleeting, so trivial in contrast to the eternal, which is all around us and which beckons us – even if with nothing more than the idea itself, especially when we wake up, half asleep but startled, blood pumping frightfully at the knowledge that one day we'll be gone while the idea remains!

And yet…the cross has made eternity more than just an idea….The cross has made it gift for us, more real than everything in the world, because everything in the world wears away. It is as if each turn of the earth on its axis, each revolution around the sun, grinds all things slowly into the ground and leaves only the gift, as eternal as the Giver, the God who cannot lie, who through sacrifice of Himself has made us a way to escape the fate from which there is (as Sartre wrote) no exit, but from which Jesus says, "I am the door" (Jn. 10:9) and promises all who step through it eternal life.

Either He is, or He isn't; either we do, or we don't.[232]

Bottom line: If the atheist is right about believing that there is no God (which honestly, is not supported by today's cosmological and anthropic evidence), then it doesn't make any difference between the atheist and the believer, between Mother Theresa and Hitler, between the Columbine and Virginia Tech

---

[232] Goldstein, *God, Gödel and Grace*, pp. 108-111.

shooters and their victims, between a saint and a monster, there's no winners and losers – just losers and losers – losers to the tug of death. If the Christian is right about his/her God (which, today's honest atheists in their sober moments uncomfortably admit that the cosmological and anthropic evidence points to), then it does make a big difference: the difference is between eternal nothingness and eternal life. The believer, therefore, doesn't lose anything or to anybody for believing that Christ has saved him/her from eternal death. For to believe otherwise is like betting your life in a gamble, where the only outcomes are lose and lose.

Chapter Twelve: Conclusion / Epilogue

index of names

Altman, Dr. Rochelle I. S.	68, 111
Arlandson, Dr. James Malcolm	133
Bacchiocchi, Dr. Samuele	93
Barnes, Dr. Ian	112
Bauckham, Dr. Richard	72, 73
Bein Amos	121
Bock, Dr. Darrell L.	85, 103, 122, 127
Bovon, Francois	47, 48, 90, 91, 92, 142, 143
Cameron, James	6, 12, 13, 14, 15, 16, 17, 19, 20, 21, 22, 29, 56, 57, 63, 64, 101, 131, 133, 134, 135, 136, 137, 138, 139, 144
Cannon, Dr. Dale M	34, 61
Caruso, Steve	69, 70
Clarke, Arthur C.	21
Crossan, John Dominic	21, 34, 57, 62, 63
Evans, Dr. Craig	63, 91, 93
Feuerverger, Dr. Andrey	50, 51, 97, 101, 105, 106
Gat, Joseph	31, 32
Geraty, Dr. Lawrence T.	83, 84
Gibson, Shimon	31, 53, 63, 126
Golan, Oded	23, 28, 53, 54, 119, 124, 125, 126, 129
Habermas, Dr. Gary R.	135
Hassan, Crown Prince of Jordan	83
Heiser, Dr. Michael S.	34, 63
Huggins, Dr. Ronald V.	90
Ingermanson, Dr. Randy	102, 104
Jacobovici, Simcha	15, 16, 20, 22, 23, 24, 39, 41, 57, 61, 63, 64, 67, 89, 91, 92, 101, 115, 119, 126, 135
Johnson, Dr. Kevin D.	34, 61
Kloner, Dr. Amos	31, 32, 33, 42, 62, 63, 68, 71, 99, 111, 123, 124, 126, 127, 142
Koppel, Ted	114

Lemche, Dr. Niels Peter	34, 61
Magness, Dr. Jodi	16, 78, 79, 81
Maier, Dr. Paul L.	77, 80, 81
Matheson, Dr. Carney	52, 113, 114, 117
Metzger, Dr. Bruce M.	133, 134
Moore Cross, Dr. Frank	42, 68
Neiger, Motti	34
Pellegrino, Dr. Charles	15, 20, 22, 24, 25, 39, 57, 63, 64, 99, 102, 109, 114, 115
Pfann, Dr. Stephen J.	51, 68, 69, 71, 72, 89, 111, 142
Poirier, Jack	102
Puech, Dr. Emile	70
Rahmani, Levy Yitzhak	33, 63, 67, 68, 71, 72, 74, 75, 78, 111, 142
Reed, Dr. Jonathan L.	34, 62, 63, 95, 145
Richards, Gerald	125
Rollston, Dr. Christopher A.	82
Shea, Dr. William H.	93
Strobel, Lee	134
Tabor, Dr. James	25, 26, 34, 41, 46, 54, 57, 61, 62, 64, 81, 102, 114, 122, 123, 125, 127
White, Dr. James	113
Witherington, Dr. Ben	73, 89
Yardeni, Dr. Ada	70
Zias, Joe	34, 61, 79, 121, 122, 127, 130

index of subjects

Acts of Philip	43, 47, 48, 49, 90, 91, 92, 93, 94, 96, 100, 101, 142
Aliens	20
Aramaic	32, 42, 43, 48, 49, 53, 56, 69, 73, 75, 90, 133
Archaeology	16, 23, 24, 34, 39, 79, 83, 93, 110, 119, 121, 122
Archaeologist	127
Atiquot	32, 33, 42, 52, 62, 68, 69, 71, 99, 111, 123, 126, 127
BBC	6, 33, 34, 35, 36, 62, 142
Bias	13, 19, 26, 27, 50, 52, 65, 67, 92, 94, 99, 100, 105, 137, 142, 144
Biblical Archaeology Review	23
Biblical Archaeology Society	119
Caesar	84, 85, 136
Caesarea	81
Chain of Custody	111
Christianity	5, 6, 12, 15, 16, 20, 25, 26, 27, 35, 63, 92, 138, 141, 144
Consumer Reports	16
Crucifixion	12, 13, 53, 56, 84, 85, 94, 136, 137
DNA	15, 51, 52, 53, 63, 84, 100, 103, 109, 110, 111, 112, 113, 114, 115, 116, 117, 120, 143, 144
Dead Sea Scrolls	26, 61, 62
Discovery Channel	24, 40, 42, 44, 45, 46, 48, 50, 53, 54, 55, 57, 59, 82, 107, 114, 119, 120, 122, 126, 131, 137
Double Standard	94
Eusebius	81
FBI	14, 125, 130
Fallacy	139
Galilee	48, 77, 79, 81, 84

Index

Geological Survey of Israel [or GSI]	120, 121
Gospel of Thomas	46
Greek	25, 32, 42, 43, 48, 56, 71, 72, 89, 90, 91, 133, 134
Heart of the Matter	33, 36, 62
Hebrew	22, 25, 26, 27, 32, 34, 42, 48, 61, 70, 71
Hebrew University	26, 34, 61
History Channel	23
Inscription	23, 28, 32, 35, 41, 42, 43, 44, 45, 47, 48, 49, 53, 54, 63, 67, 68, 69, 70, 71, 72, 73, 76, 77, 78, 79, 80, 81, 82, 84, 87, 89, 90, 99, 102, 119, 120, 121, 125, 127, 142
Instrument	69, 76, 87
Israel Antiquities Authority/IAA	23, 31, 53, 54, 63, 69, 79, 119, 126, 129
James, Brother of Jesus/ James ossuary	23, 28, 45, 53, 54, 55, 68, 80, 82, 89, 100, 111, 119, 120, 121, 122, 123, 124, 125, 126, 127, 129, 130, 144
Jerusalem	15, 16, 26, 31, 44, 45, 46, 47, 48, 49, 50, 52, 53, 56, 57, 61, 62, 69, 70, 77, 78, 80, 81, 83, 86, 89, 90, 91, 92, 98, 104, 106, 109, 112, 119, 121, 122, 126, 142
Jesus	6, 9, 10, 11, 12, 13, 14, 15, 16, 17, 19, 20, 22, 23, 24, 25, 26, 27, 28, 29, 32, 33, 34, 35, 36, 37, 39, 40, 41, 42, 43, 44, 45, 46, 47, 48, 49, 50, 51, 52, 53, 54, 55, 56, 57, 61, 62, 63, 64, 65, 66, 67, 68, 69, 70, 71, 73, 76, 77, 78, 79, 80, 81, 82, 83, 84, 85, 86, 87, 88, 89, 90, 91, 92, 94, 97, 98, 99, 100, 101, 102, 103, 104, 105, 109, 110, 113, 114, 115, 116, 119, 120, 121, 122, 123, 126, 127, 128, 131, 132, 133, 134, 135, 136, 137, 138, 139, 141, 142, 143, 144, 145
Jesus Dynasty, The	25, 114

Jesus Family Tomb, The	6, 19, 22, 35, 39, 41, 42, 43, 46, 47, 48, 49, 51, 56, 62, 63, 64, 65, 67, 70, 71, 73, 77, 80, 84, 86, 90, 92, 97, 98, 99, 100, 101, 102, 103, 104, 105, 109, 110, 113, 114, 115, 119, 120, 123, 127, 128, 131, 132, 133, 134, 135, 138, 141, 142, 143, 144
Joseph	11, 26, 31, 32, 33, 41, 42, 43, 44, 45, 49, 50, 53, 54, 55, 61, 67, 68, 70, 76, 77, 78, 79, 80, 85, 86, 87, 91, 99, 103, 104, 105, 119, 120, 121, 122, 126, 127, 134, 135, 136
Josephus	11, 12, 78, 91, 134, 135, 136
Kokhim	32, 37
Looters	32, 110
Looted	76, 87, 117
Lost Tomb of Jesus, The	17, 19, 20, 22, 23, 24, 26, 29, 35, 39, 40, 41, 42, 44, 45, 46, 48, 50, 52, 53, 54, 55, 57, 63, 64, 70, 71, 73, 77, 82, 90, 91, 92, 95, 97, 98, 103, 105, 109, 110, 114, 119, 120, 121, 122, 126, 131, 137, 138, 141, 142, 144
Manuscript/Manuscripts	90, 133, 134, 138
Maria	32, 44, 47, 81, 91, 104
Mariamene	32, 33, 42, 45, 47, 48, 49, 50, 51, 67, 71, 73, 75, 89, 90, 94, 100, 101, 102, 112, 114, 115, 142, 143
Martha	32, 33, 49, 71, 72, 73, 78, 111
Mary	26, 32, 33, 42, 43, 44, 45, 47, 48, 49, 50, 51, 52, 53, 63, 67, 71, 72, 73, 78, 79, 80, 81, 82, 86, 89, 90, 91, 92, 93, 94, 96, 99, 100, 101, 102, 103, 105, 131, 137, 142, 143
Marya	32, 44, 50
Maryah	82, 83
Matya	32, 33, 45, 50, 80, 81, 82, 102, 103, 105, 114, 137
Migdal	89, 90
Multigenerational	82, 83, 104, 108, 114
Nazareth	11, 14, 15, 26, 48, 51, 63, 66, 73, 77, 78, 79, 80, 82, 86, 99, 100, 102, 103, 109, 116, 127, 144

Index

New Testament	11, 19, 45, 46, 48, 56, 57, 63, 72, 73, 84, 85, 89, 91, 94, 97, 99, 115, 119, 131, 132, 133, 134, 135, 136, 137, 138, 144
New York Times, The	21
Orion Center	26, 34, 61, 62
Ossuary	15, 23, 26, 28, 32, 33, 34, 35, 41, 42, 43, 44, 46, 47, 53, 54, 55, 56, 57, 62, 67, 68, 71, 72, 73, 75, 77, 78, 79, 80, 82, 84, 85, 89, 90, 94, 100, 101, 102, 103, 108, 110, 111, 115, 119, 120, 121, 122, 123, 124, 125, 126, 127, 129, 130, 137, 143, 144
Patina	55, 63, 120, 121, 122, 126, 130
Peer Review	16, 17, 27
Return to Sodom and Gomorrah	24
Rome	46, 84, 85
Scientific American	101, 105
Special Pleading	80, 102, 103, 124, 138
Statistics	50, 63, 97, 101, 102
Sunday Times	33, 34, 36, 62
Talpiot	31, 32, 33, 34, 35, 36, 39, 40, 41, 43, 45, 46, 47, 49, 50, 51, 53, 54, 55, 56, 57, 59, 61, 62, 63, 64, 66, 67, 68, 71, 77, 79, 81, 82, 83, 84, 89, 91, 92, 94, 98, 99, 100, 101, 102, 104, 105, 111, 116, 119, 120, 122, 124, 126, 130, 138, 141, 142, 143, 144, 145
Tel Megiddo	82
Terminator, The	20
Tiberias	84
Titanic	15, 20, 21, 24
Tomb	6, 12, 14, 15, 17, 19, 20, 22, 23, 24, 26, 29, 31, 32, 33, 34, 35, 36, 39, 40, 41, 42, 43, 44, 45, 46, 47, 48, 49, 50, 51, 52, 53, 54, 55, 56, 57, 59, 61, 62, 63, 64, 65, 66, 67, 68, 69, 70, 71, 73, 76, 77, 78, 79, 80, 81, 82, 83, 84, 85, 86, 87, 89, 90, 91, 92, 94, 97, 98, 99, 100, 101, 102, 103, 104, 105, 106, 108, 109, 110, 111, 112, 113, 114, 115, 116, 117, 119, 120, 121, 122, 123, 124, 126, 127, 128, 130, 131, 132, 133, 134, 135, 137, 138, 139, 141, 142, 143, 144, 145

Tzippori	84
Vandals	32, 110, 111, 143
Vandalized	76, 87, 117
Volcanoes of the Deep Sea	21
Yehuda	32, 33, 45, 68, 69, 82, 83, 101, 102, 105, 115, 137
Yeshua	32, 33, 41, 42, 44, 45, 46, 53, 54, 67, 68, 69, 70, 71, 73, 74, 77, 78, 79, 80, 82, 83, 99, 100, 101, 102, 103, 105, 112, 114, 115, 119, 142
Yose	32, 33, 44, 45, 50, 80, 99, 100, 101, 103, 104, 105, 115, 137, 142

list of illustrations

Christ Bearing His Cross by H. Hofmann	4
Jewish Tomb at El-Messahney by Byram	18
James, Brother of Jesus by P. Paradiso	28
Ancient Jerusalem by L.N. Rosenthal	29
The Tomb That Dare Not Speak Its Name by Sunday Times	36
Tomb of the Kings by Byram	37
Talpiot Tomb Entrance 1980 by PR Newswire	59
Yeshua Inscription by L.Y. Rahmani	74
Yeshua bar Joseph by Aramaic Designs	75
Mariamene inscription by L.Y. Rahmani	75
David's Judgment Seat, Jerusalem by Félix Bonfils	87
Statistics Formula by Discovery Channel	107
Mitochondrial DNA Tree by BassettDNA	117
James Ossuary Throne by Israel Antiquities Authority	129
Erasmus, The Scholar by Holbein d. J., Hans	139
Jesus Ascension by Standard Pub Co	146

acknowledgements

I would like to acknowledge, dedicate, and deeply thank the various people, who without their help, this book would not exist.

My Family:
- *Jesus.* The Lamb that was slain from the foundation of the world.
- *Wife and daughter.* My wife Jen, whose patience and love has been a source of strength. My daughter Kaycee, who is the apple of my eye, a constant source of happiness in our home.
- *Parents.* To my father, Dr. Diego Sausa, who has always given me guidance not only in my writings but in my life. To my mother, Dr. Maruja Sausa, who is a shining example of humility and what a biblical servant should be.
- *My siblings.* Trish and Stacey for their tenacious ability to pepper me with questions while I'm working, which fortunately gave me much needed mental breaks.
- *Ortiz Church.* To my friends and colleagues at the Ortiz Church in Fort Myers, who I consider to be a part of my family.

The Vision Press and Associates
- Thanks to the editors that worked so hard for this project:
    - Dr. Jeffrey Clark (General Editor)
    - Jody Ortiz (Layout Editor)

Experts:
- The following is a list of individuals in their respective field of academics that I would like to personally thank them for their time:
    - DNA/Forensics:
        - Dr. Ian Barnes
    - Archaeology:
        - Dr. Lawrence Geraty
        - Jennifer Groves
        - Dr. Jodi Magness
        - Dr. William Shea
        - Dr. Randall W. Younker
        - Joe Zias
    - Documentary Related:
        - Dr. Tal Ilan
        - Dr. James Tabor
    - FBI Related:
        - Special Agent Ann Todd
        - Retired Special Agent Gerald B. Richards
    - History/New Testament:
        - Dr. Samuele Bacchiocchi

- Dr. François Bovon
- Dr. Craig Evans
- Dr. Paul Maier
- Dr. Ben Witherington
  - Inscriptions:
    - Dr. Rochelle I. Altman
    - Steve Caruso
    - Dr. Doug Gropp
    - Dr. Michael Heiser
    - Dr. Stephen Pfann
  - Statistics:
    - Professor Richard G. Brown

supplemental materials

Supplemental materials are available online at our web site:

www.JesusTombReview.com

Find additional articles, interviews, news updates, videos, and other resources you can use for study groups, and sermons.

We want to hear from you.
Please send your comments about this book to us in care of
support@thevisionpress.com. Thank you.

[tvp]

The Vision Press
690029 Daniels Pkwy #147
Fort Myers, FL 33912

www.ingramcontent.com/pod-product-compliance
Lightning Source LLC
Chambersburg PA
CBHW070918180426
43192CB00038B/1753